Mary Fuller

PAULINE

Napoleon's Favourite Sister

PAULINE

NAPOLEON'S FAVOURITE SISTER

Pierson Dixon

COLLINS
St James's Place, London

First Impression   November 1964
Second Impression   September 1966

For Ismene

Preface

PAULINE BONAPARTE BOUGHT THE HÔTEL DE CHAROST
in the rue du Faubourg St. Honoré in 1803 and sold it to the
British Government on October 24, 1814, since when it has
been the British Embassy in Paris. Living in this historic house,
which 150 years later is much as it was after Pauline enlarged,
redecorated and furnished it in the Empire style, I was tempted
to write something about its previous owner. The fine library
presented to the Embassy by one of my predecessors, the first
Viscount Norwich, contained a nucleus of source books easy
to hand. If the book goes in some detail into Pauline Bonaparte's
household arrangements, it is because I thought that British
readers might be interested to know about one of our finest
official residences abroad.

Pauline's life is inseparable from the rise and fall of Napoleon
and the success story of the Bonaparte family. Her own fortunes
had a direct and continuous connection with the career of
Napoleon, who, even after his fall from power, remained
uppermost in her thoughts. I have therefore tried to set her
life against the background of the stirring events through which
she lived and to bring out the extent to which Napoleon affected
it. In doing this I have consulted both English and French
authorities on Napoleon and his times, leaning perhaps towards
French sources as these were more accessible to me in Paris,
where most of this book was written.

39, rue du Faubourg St. Honoré,
Paris. April 1964

JOSEPH (Giuseppe)	NAPOLEON (Napoleone)	LUCIEN (Lucciano)	ELISA (Maria-Anna)
b. 7 Jan. 1768	b. 15 Aug. 1769	b. 21 Mar. 1775	b. 3 Jan. 1777
d. 7 Apr. 1845	d. 5 May 1821	d. 25 Jun. 1840	d. 7 Aug. 1820
m. 1 Aug. 1794 Marie-Julie Clary (1777–1845). 2 daughters	m. (1) 9 Mar. 1796 Marie-Joséphine-Rose Tascher de la Pagerie, widow of Vicomte de Beauharnais (1763-1814). No issue	m. (1) 15 May 1794 Catherine Boyer (1773-1800). 2 daughters	m. 5 May 1797 Felix Bacciochi (1762-1841). 3 sons
King of Naples, 30 Mar. 1806. King of Spain, 13 May 1808	By her first marriage Joséphine had two children: Eugène de Beauharnais, and Eugénie-Hortense who married Louis Bonaparte	m. (2) 1803 Marie-Alexandrine de Bleschamps, divorced wife of M. Jouberthon (1778-1855). 6 sons, 4 daughters	Grand Duchess of Lucca, June 1805, and later of Parma and Piacenza
	m. (2) 1 Apr. 1810 Maria Luisa, Archduchess of Austria (1791-1847). 1 son, King of Rome, later Duke of Reichstadt b. 20 Mar. 1811, d. 20 Jul. 1832	Lucien and his descendants were disbarred by Napoleon from the succession	

ETIZIA RAMOLINO (1750-1836)

IS (gi)	PAULINE (Maria-Paola)	CAROLINE (Maria-Annunziata)	JÉRÔME (Girolamo)
Sep. 1778	b. 20 Oct. 1780	b. 25 Mar. 1782	b. 15 Nov. 1784
5 Jul. 1846	d. 9 Jun. 1825	d. 18 May 1839	d. 24 Jun. 1860

IS (gi)

Sep. 1778
5 Jul. 1846

Jan. 1802
énie-
tense de
uharnais (1783-
7), daughter of
phine by her
husband. She
3 sons. The
st died in
ncy, the second
l without issue
1 after his
riage, and the
d became the
peror
oleon III.

is was made
g of Holland,
ne 1806 and
icated 1 July
o

PAULINE (Maria-Paola)

b. 20 Oct. 1780
d. 9 Jun. 1825

m. (1) 14 Jun. 1797
Victor Emmanuel
Leclerc
(1772-1802).
1 son (Dermid),
b. 20 Apr. 1798,
d. 14 Aug. 1804

m. (2) 28 Aug. 1803
Prince Camillo
Borghese
(1775-1832)
No issue

CAROLINE (Maria-Annunziata)

b. 25 Mar. 1782
d. 18 May 1839

m. 20 Jan. 1800
Joachim Murat
2 sons,
2 daughters

Grand Duchess of
Berg and Cleves,
30 Mar. 1806.
Murat succeeded
Joseph as King of
Naples in 1808, and
was executed in
1815

JÉRÔME (Girolamo)

b. 15 Nov. 1784
d. 24 Jun. 1860

m. (1) 24 Dec. 1803
Miss Elizabeth
Patterson
(1785-1879).
1 son

Marriage annulled

m. (2) 22 Aug. 1807
Princess Catherine
of Württemberg
(1783-1826).
2 sons,
1 daughter

From the younger
son, Prince Napoleon
Joseph (b. 1822),
descends the present
head of the family,
Prince Napoleon
(b. 1914)

Contents

Contents

Illustrations

I

Fancy Clear

I. Paoletta

1786-96

THE PORT OF AJACCIO SLUMBERED IN THE SEPTEMBER
sunshine of 1786 and the shutters of the tall, gaunt house in the
Strada Malherba were closed against the heat of the day. Inside,
there was movement and animation. The chatter and shrieks in
Italian of children of different ages filled the house. In the
darkened dining hall a handsome olive-skinned woman in her
late thirties was calmly directing the arrangment of a dining-
table. Letizia Buonaparte, a widow for the past year, was
preparing for the return of her second son, Napoleone, who
had been away from his native Corsica for more than seven
years. Her stern and prematurely careworn features relaxed at
the prospect of seeing this favourite son, who a year ago had
received his commission as sub-lieutenant of artillery.

Napoleone Buonaparte owed his military career to his father,
Carlo, who, for all his fecklessness and extravagance, had
contrived to obtain recognition by the French State of the
aristocratic status of the family and on the strength of that a free
cadetship for Napoleone at the military school of Brienne in
Champagne. From Brienne Napoleone had proceeded to the
military academy at Paris.

Since her husband's death in 1785 Signora Buonaparte had
been constantly worried about the problem of giving her children
the upbringing and education that he and she were determined
they should have. The Buonapartes, an old and proud family
who had been in Corsica since their migration from Italy in the
early sixteenth century, had a leading position in the island. But
they had never been wealthy, Corsica was a poor country, and
politics had always seemed more important to a Buonaparte than

riches. Letizia was not to know that within thirteen years Napoleone would be the ruler of France and the Buonapartes the most powerful family in Europe.

Carlo Buonaparte and Letizia Ramolino had had eight children. The eldest son, Giuseppe—or Joseph, since all the Buonapartes, except Letizia herself, gallicised their names after the family was established in France—was a quiet youth of eighteen. Lucciano (Lucien), even at eleven was a highly individual and brilliant boy. Eight-year-old Luigi (Louis), intelligent and wayward, and two-year-old Girolamo (Jérôme), the youngest of the eight children, completed the boys. Of the three little girls, Maria-Anna (Elisa) was the eldest and remained the most Corsican of the family, and the youngest was Maria-Annunziata (Caroline).

Pauline Bonaparte, the future Princess Pauline Borghese, was the second daughter. She had been baptised Maria-Paola, but was known in the family as Paoletta. She was born at Ajaccio on October 20, 1780, and had thus never seen Napoleon, who had left Corsica for school in France in April of the previous year. Graceful and vivacious, she was her mother's favourite. Letizia, who herself undertook the education at home of the younger children (except Elisa who obtained a scholarship at the school at Saint Cyr founded by Madame de Maintenon for indigent girls of noble birth), certainly did little to correct Paoletta's marked distaste for study and her early predilection for pretty clothes and pranks. She amused her indulgent mother and was allowed to run wild in and out of the house.

Napoleon, on his return to Corsica in September 1786, had just turned seventeen. There is some controversy about the date of Napoleon's birth; but since his elder brother Joseph was born in January 1768, Napoleon could not have been born in February of the same year, as he claimed at the time of his marriage with Joséphine, and therefore the date he subsequently gave of August 15, 1769, is generally accepted. He is described as being at this time short, dark, pale and extremely thin. Full of the new ideas that were fermenting in the years just before the Revolution, he was already intense and assertive. The realistic side of his forceful character was manifesting itself too at this early age: he had electrified the officers of the eighteenth-century military academy by presenting them with a memorandum criticising its shortcomings and proposing reforms. What first impression this elder brother made on the six-year-old Paoletta is not known—this slim, emaciated young man, with the piercing blue eyes darting out of pallid bony features, swaggering a little in his sombre, tightly-cut lieutenant's uniform, but she was undoubtedly under his spell all her life. He forbade and arranged her marriages, kept a close eye on her extravagances and protected her from scandal. This was often done, no doubt, for the sake of the prestige of the ruling House, but also from real affection. For all her capriciousness she repaid him amply, with the loyalty of a subject and the devotion of a sister. Their complex relations are the clue to Pauline's complex life.

This dynamic, acquisitive, opportunist family, Italian by race and culture, Corsican in its standards of family honour, was to dominate France for fifteen years under the eagle wing of the most remarkable of the sons—unless Lucien is to be considered even more remarkable than Napoleon Bonaparte, for his was the decisiveness and coolness which, at a moment of great peril, brought off the successful *coup d'état* which made Napoleon ruler of France. Alone among the brothers and sisters he felt scruples about Napoleon assuming the throne, or perhaps it was less a question of scruple than of personal vanity. How could the king-maker bear to be a mere subject? He contracted two marriages of affection and scornfully refused to fall in with his brother's dynastic plans and divorce his humdrum second wife, thus forfeiting a throne and losing all political influence under the Empire.

The rest of the family, with varying good grace, accepted Napoleon's plans for their marriages and their future. All, in varying degrees of zest, entered into the heady business of leading the new Napoleonic society and posturing at the pinnacle of the new French Empire. All cajoled, exploited and blackmailed Napoleon. Except Pauline, the most irresponsible, the most capricious of the clan, who retained a deep sense of loyalty to her brother and alone of the brothers and sisters stood by him in defeat. None of them was immune to the intoxication of success and power. Except Signora Letizia. She never lost her sense of proportion. Inured from early youth to the vicissitudes of life, she retained till her death twenty-one years after Napoleon's fall her mistrust of success and its splendours and her severe standards of simplicity in behaviour, dress and general outlook on life. She will for ever be remembered for the classic remark, in her broad Corsican French, *"Pourvou que cela doure."*

The Bonapartes were brought up as Corsicans, Italian was their native language. Napoleon only learnt to speak French at school at Brienne and to the end of his days made mistakes in French orthography. In the family circle, even in the days of greatness, Italian—perhaps out of deference to Signora Letizia—was the language they preferred to talk, though Napoleon's Italian, according to his private secretary, was poor. "I left Corsica too young to be able to express myself easily in Italian," he remarked as a young man, according to one of the family's Corsican friends, the future Duchesse d'Abrantès.

The rise of the family was swift and, as seen against the backdrop of history and the extraordinary capacities of Napoleon, inevitable. But it did not happen in a flash and there were moments of desperation and disaster. It remains a miracle that this Italian family, long settled in an island which only became French (on annexation from the Genoese) a few months before Napoleon's birth in 1769, was able to assert its dominance over France and the destinies of the French nation.

The fall of the Bastille on July 14, 1789, touched off an explosion of history without which the Bonaparte family must have remained obscure and even the genius of Napoleon would have spent itself against a firmly established order of events. This extraordinary political convulsion provided the circumstances in which a man of extraordinary talents was able to seize supreme power. Even so, it was some time before Napoleon was presented with his first opportunity to make his reputation. During the first four years of the Revolution he paid several visits to Corsica, where power had been seized by the Corsican patriot, Paoli. Paoli, who stood for the independence of Corsica, regarded the acquisition of the island by France as treachery and the Republic as an offence. He was fond of the English, who had been kind to him during his exile under the Monarchy, and knew that in present circumstances he could rely on their support in his struggle to sever the union with France.

The Bonapartes, inspired by Napoleon, were enthusiastic for the French connection and the Revolution. Napoleon insulted the old patriot in a public manifesto, calling him a political charlatan. The pro-French enthusiasts, in a country where feuds are second nature, rallied to the Bonapartes, who, amid rising tempers, became the acknowledged leaders of the French faction. Signora Letizia kept the family house in Ajaccio as its stronghold and headquarters. But nothing went well for the Bonapartes. Paoli, supported by the British, maintained his ascendancy. The Revolutionary Government in France was too preoccupied with affairs at home to provide efficient help for its supporters in distant Corsica. The French Republic was proclaimed in September 1792 and Louis XVI was executed the following January.

During the night of May 13, 1793, the Paolists swooped on Ajaccio. Napoleon was in the north, with Joseph. He had managed to send his mother a warning message a few days before: "Get ready to leave; this country is not for us." The Signora made plans for instant flight. It was time, for a few hours later the Paolists entered and sacked the family mansion. During the night, with Paoletta, four of her other children and her half-brother Fesch, she took to the hills to the north of Ajaccio. After several hours' hard walking across the *maquis*, they came to the Bonaparte property of Milelli and rested during the day. From there, through the night, they made their way to the east and south, circling the Gulf of Ajaccio, to the Tower of Capitello on the edge of the Campo de Oro, the modern airport of Ajaccio.

There they had not long to wait. The small fleet of the Commissioners of the Republic was approaching, with Napoleon and Joseph on board. The two brothers discerned people waving from the Tower. Lowering a small boat, they advanced to investigate. On seeing his mother, Napoleon leapt from the boat and swam and splashed through the waves to the shore. The family were taken on board and sailed to Calvi in the northwest of the island. Shortly afterwards the Signora and her children sailed for Toulon in a merchant ship which safely ran the gauntlet of the English patrols.

Toulon when they reached it was in flames. The inhabitants, infuriated by the excesses of the Revolutionary Government, had revolted, proclaimed the King and called in the English and Spanish fleets. By August the great arsenal and fortress was in the hands of the English. This was Napoleon's chance. His reputation as a promising young artilleryman was remembered and he found himself in command, with promotion to lieutenant-colonel, of the artillery which formed part of the reinforcements rushed to Toulon by the French Government. By December, the fortress was recaptured and the English expelled. Napoleon had won his spurs.

The chaotic and dangerous conditions in Toulon made it no place for a young family. The Signora accordingly took the five young children along the coast and finally established herself in Marseille. Marseille, though not in a state of war, was in a state of Terror. Arrests and executions were the order of the day. The indomitable Signora, practically penniless, found a cheap dwelling on the top floor of a poor house near the old Port at the foot of the Cannebière and set her daughters to work as laundresses. The three girls, high-spirited and attractive, were thus brought in contact with some of the well-to-do families of Marseille. One in particular, the Clary family, took pity on the exiles. The following year (1794) Joseph, the eldest of the Bonapartes, married Julie Clary who was to become queen of Spain. Her sister, Désirée, married Marshal Bernadotte and thus became queen of Sweden. All trace of the Clary family mansion was obliterated under the German bombardment of the old Port in the Second World War.

Paoletta, or Paulette as she came to be known about this time, was nearly thirteen in the summer of 1793. Her elder sister Maria-Anna (Elisa) was seventeen, and the younger sister Maria-Annunziata (Caroline) eleven. In later years the enemies of the family, besides mocking the menial occupation of the Bonaparte girls at this period, alleged that the Signora was reduced to such straits that she allowed her rich clients to take unwonted liberties with them. Many of the stories were invented and circulated by the Bourbons or the English as anti-Napoleonic propaganda at the height of Napoleon's power and after the Bourbon restoration. One of the most libellous accounts is by the Englishman Lewis Goldsmith, who published a pamphlet in 1815: *The Secret History of the Cabinet of Napoleon Bonaparte and the Court of St. Cloud.* Goldsmith stated plainly: "Madame Bonaparte kept *maison ouverte* at Marseille for her own daughters; owing to her scandalous conduct she was finally ordered by the police to leave the town." None of this is true. But it does appear from the memoirs of friends and acquaintances of the family at this time that the two elder Bonaparte girls had a reputation for a certain free-and-easy way of living and did not always keep good company. Writing many years later, General de Ricard, who lived in Marseille and knew the family well, defends the reputation of the Bonaparte girls but feels bound to admit that "opinion at Marseille was not favourably disposed towards them and believed that they indulged in adventures of a gallant and even scandalous kind." Perhaps it was only something less than the demure behaviour expected of young ladies before the revolutionary years inevitably lowered standards.

Napoleon's success at Toulon and his promotion to brigadier-general eased the position of the family, and with the arrival in Marseille of two Commissioners of the Republic, Barras and Fréron, their situation was further improved. Signora Letizia was able to persuade the Commissioners to grant her a pension as a Corsican patriot, and to move to more comfortable quarters.

In 1794 Napoleon himself established his headquarters first at Marseille, later at Nice, as commander of the artillery of the Army of Italy. The fall of Robespierre and the end of the Terror in July brought quieter times to France but difficulties for the Bonaparte family. Napoleon had become identified with the Terrorists and was in disfavour when the reaction set in. For a few weeks he was under arrest. But he had a powerful protector in Barras, one of the Directory of Five which now ruled the country, and who had been struck by the young commander's ability.

2. The Business of Paulette

1794-6

WHEN HER BROTHER JOSEPH MARRIED MADEMOISELLE Clary in August 1794 Paulette was nearly fourteen. The event made a great impression on the precocious young woman, who recalled that this was about the age at which her mother had married her father. She too wanted to get married. It was not that she had any particular man in mind. It was not that she had reflected on life and decided that the married state was an ideal to which one should aspire at the earliest possible moment. Paulette never gave any profound reflection to anything. It was simply that she knew herself to be pretty and imagined that marriage was desirable in itself. She wanted to be *dans le mouvement*.

Paulette must have been very fetching at this age, with the gamine and coltish gestures, the dancing eyes and the glowing youthfulness which all the gossips and memorialists recalled when her brother became famous and everybody talked about the Bonapartes. She was hardly educated, but she could express herself vividly and, when necessary, with force. She learnt French, and spoke and wrote it fluently, although in moments of emotion she turned naturally to her native Italian. She was made for gaiety and happiness. Soon to be engulfed in an overwhelming tide of history, all she knew at fourteen was that life was suddenly wonderful. There was money and comfort such as she had never known. Something was happening to her youthful world, something to do with the brother who was her idol. Everything was strange, exciting and new.

If Paulette was sexually precocious, it was a prophetic precocity. Her behaviour at fourteen foreshadowed the short career

of the adult Pauline. Amorous by nature, flirtatious by temperament, she lived for frivolity, but this frivolity was balanced by a
gaiety and good nature which charmed most of her acquaintance and by a quality of courage and loyalty which endeared
her to her great brother and led him constantly to condone
extravagances which must often have been politically embarrassing as well as exasperating. Pauline rarely had a serious
thought in her head, but she never did any human being serious
harm.

In these early days Napoleon automatically assumed the rôle
he was to fulfil all his life in forbidding and arranging his sister's
affairs of the heart. She wanted to marry a certain Billon, a
soap-merchant of Marseille. Napoleon vetoed the match.
"A certain Citizen Billon, whom I am assured you know," he
wrote to his brother Joseph, "has asked for Paulette's hand; this
citizen has no money. I have written to Mama that it cannot
be considered." It is, however, clear that about this time he was
considering a suitable match for his precocious young sister. An
officer on Napoleon's staff, Junot, next presented himself as
suitor. Paulette was willing enough, but Napoleon persuaded
his aide-de-camp to forget about it as he had no money. "You
have nothing, Paulette has nothing. Total, nothing." The future
General consoled himself by marrying a few years later Mademoiselle Laure Permon, daughter of a Greek-Corsican family
intimate with the Bonapartes in Ajaccio, who with her husband's
ascent to relative fame under the Empire became Duchesse
d'Abrantès. Laure, four years younger than Paulette, knew her
intimately and lived in the inner group which surrounded
Napoleon during his rise to power. The memoirs which she
wrote in later life are packed with incidents and stories about
Paulette. Though diffuse and gossipy, and often to be taken with
a grain of salt, they give a vivid and generally authentic picture
of Napoleon's family circle. It is clear that Mademoiselle Permon
disapproved of Mademoiselle Bonaparte. Their marriages made
her the more critical. Young Madame Junot was thoroughly
jealous of Princess Pauline Borghese. This bias, accentuated by

affection for the great Napoleon, means that the Duchesse d'Abrantès's recollections of her girlhood friend must be treated with considerable reserve. Yet Laure Permon was a person of quality. She was intelligent and often gave Paulette excellent advice (which she rarely followed). Immensely observant, she was a born recorder. Very little escaped her, whether the weaknesses in the character of her innumerable friends, or the trends of the newest fashion in clothes. One has the feeling, reading her informative and often malicious account of the Bonapartes in their heyday, that she regarded them as parvenus: she could never forget that her Greek mother was a Comnenos, descended from an Imperial line far older and more authentic than that of the new rulers of France.

Of the two Commissioners who had been sent to Toulon at the time of the revolt, Barras shortly returned to Paris and his key position in the administration, the other—Stanislas Fréron—stayed in Marseille as representative of the Directory in the departments of the Midi. It was these two men who had promoted Napoleon general, in the name of the people, after his part in the relief of Toulon. Both thus became well acquainted with the Bonaparte family. Barras did not forget Napoleon, and Fréron became infatuated with Paulette.

In Paris, by the autumn of 1795 a strong movement of conservative reaction, released by the fall of Robespierre and the end of the Terror, was threatening the position of the Convention and the Directory of Five, in whom the executive power of the Republic was vested. The Convention charged Barras, the most influential member of the Directory, with the task of protecting the Republic against the insurrection which threatened to break out and appointed him commander-in-chief of the Army of the Interior. Barras, no soldier, made Napoleon commander of the troops in Paris. On October 4, 1795 (famous as the 13th of Vendémiaire of the year IV), Napoleon, firing a few rounds of grape into the counter-revolutionaries marching in massed crowds towards the Assembly building, crushed the incipient insurrection at a blow. He was rewarded by promotion

to the rank of Artillery Divisional General and appointed
General-in-Chief of the Army of the Interior.

Meanwhile in Marseille, in the New Year, Fréron formally
asked for Paulette's hand in marriage. Joseph consulted Napoleon.
"I see no objection," he replied on January 11, 1796, "if he is
rich." It is not so fantastic that Paulette at scarcely fifteen should
have been considered marriageable by her family when one
remembers that in Corsica girls habitually matured and married
very young, and the youthful Paulette was advanced even for a
Corsican damsel.

Fortunately for Paulette her mother opposed the match.
Everything known about Fréron is unsavoury. Son of a famous
eighteenth-century man of letters and journalist, he was brought
up in the great world and himself became a journalist of the
most extreme and violent kind. Climbing on to the Revolutionary band-waggon, he was sent to the south of France to deal
with the aftermath of the Toulon insurrection, which he did with
sanguinary viciousness. This evil reputation he tried to live
down on his second mission to the South as representative of
the Directory by entertaining the Marseillais on a magnificent
scale. Fréron must have had charm, he was deceptively civilised
in his personal appearance, he knew the world and the great
names of the reign of Louis XVI. That he was a libertine, a
political adventurer and a man of no principles can hardly have
been apparent even to so precocious an adolescent. Paulette did
not know that he had two children by a Mademoiselle Masson,
a lady of the Comédie Italienne, with whom he had been living
in Paris. It is not surprising that, avid for pleasure and luxury,
she was dazzled by the Proconsul's fêtes and entranced by the
admiration of this man of the world much older than herself
(he was forty-one in 1796).

Many of Paulette's letters to Fréron and Napoleon, written
between January and October 1796, have survived. They make
pathetic and indeed moving reading. The style is conventional
and, considering Paulette's haphazard upbringing, surprisingly
elegant. Mostly she wrote in French, relapsing into Italian from

time to time. Through the conventional politeness and circumlocutions there comes an authentic note of youthful passion and, as the drama played itself out to its miserable end, an adult note of despair. The girl who wrote these letters could not have been a vulgar, flirtatious adolescent superficially attracted by the first man of the world she had met. The nascent passion is genuine, the experience real and painful.

"I swear to you, dear Stanislas," she wrote in February 1796, "that I shall never love anyone but you . . . Who could oppose the union of two souls who seek only happiness and find it in mutual love? No, my friend, neither Mama nor anyone else can refuse you my hand."

This is conventional, perhaps artificial, as is the ending, in which she displays her acquaintance with classical Italian literature: "Paulette will love you as much as Petrarch loved Laura. Farewell, Stanislas, my tender friend, I salute you as I love you."

Fréron pressed his suit but was worried by the opposition of Signora Letizia. On March 24 he wrote to Napoleon (in Toulon) begging him to remove the "slight objections" of the Signora. Napoleon was embarrassed and irritated by this letter. He knew that Fréron was falling into disfavour among those who counted in Paris. His own affairs were advancing, he had just been appointed to the command of the Army of Italy, and what perhaps weighed with him more, he had only a fortnight before contracted marriage with a lady of a certain social position, Joséphine, widow of the Vicomte de Beauharnais. Decidedly he did not want his sister to contract a *mésalliance*.

The next day Napoleon arrived at Marseille to see his family before assuming command in Italy. He dined that night with Fréron, and hardly uttered a word. During a subsequent interview he temporised, leaving Fréron with the impression that he would try to persuade the Signora to agree to the marriage. But in fact his mind was made up. Shortly afterwards, from his headquarters in Italy, he fired off a series of injunctions to his mother, Joseph and Lucien. "I beg you to arrange the business of Paulette. It is not my intention that she should marry Fréron."

He also asked Barras, Fréron's colleague, to dissuade Fréron from persisting in trying to marry "a child of sixteen of whom he is old enough to be the father. One does not try to marry when one has had two children by a woman still living."

This letter was written shortly after the French victory at Lodi on May 10, 1796. During the Italian campaign against the Austrians, from the first victory at Montenotte in April to the capture of Mantua in February 1797, Napoleon managed from time to time to keep a brotherly eye on "the business of Paulette". He had dealt Fréron a shrewd blow in revealing his knowledge of his connection with Mademoiselle Masson.

Fréron, who had concealed this liaison from Paulette, now appreciated that she was bound to hear of it and decided to confess. He conveyed the information by letter. Paulette was, naturally, aghast, and indeed fell ill. But she seems to have recovered quickly, and on May 19, 1796, wrote reassuringly:

"I have just received your letter which gave me great pleasure since I was beginning to be worried by your silence; though on the other hand it upset me because of that woman. Don't worry, I am only ill because I am bored and tired. Farewell, my good friend, I love you more than myself. Farewell. Excuse my bad writing; in bed it is awkward."

As the summer wore on a note of despair begins to make itself felt in the letters. She wrote to Napoleon, but her appeals remained unanswered. The General, it is true, was fully occupied with the Austrians in north Italy, and in any case his mind was made up. On July 2, as Napoleon had just set about investing Mantua, Paulette in distant Marseille was writing to Fréron that she could not sleep, even in the country and in spite of all sorts of distractions. "You nearly lost your Paulette; I fell into the water trying to jump into a boat. Luckily I was saved in time."

She was no doubt very sorry for herself. She became ill and weak from self-pity. She added to this letter: "The water I swallowed in the river has not chilled my heart towards you"; and ended with a few lines in Italian: *Addio, anima mia ti amo sempre, mia vita* ("Goodnight, breath of my life, my eternal love"). This is Paulette in a mood of self-compassion, finding in her Italian reading-books the words to express her feelings.

Fréron's position meanwhile was deteriorating. He was increasingly unpopular and Barras, his former friend, was ready to desert him. Lucien continued to support Fréron, but Joséphine now took a hand and did her best to ensure that her sister-in-law did not marry this man who clearly had no future. This infuriated Paulette, who expressed her feelings in a letter to Fréron on July 6.

"Everybody is conspiring to frustrate us . . . All your friends are renegades, even the wife of Napoleon. But all these difficulties, far from diminishing, increase my love for you . . . Courage, my loved one . . . Shall I write to Napoleon?"

She closed in Italian on a despairing note: "I was beginning to lose heart from the frustration of all these checks, not that I doubted your sentiments. The tender assurances you give me reassure me more and more. Perhaps things will change. Love me always, my own, my dear friend, I breathe only for you, I love you."

The letters followed hot and fast. "Ah, that letter of yours, how I covered it in kisses and pressed it to my heart." In Italian: "Everything I do is for you alone. I love you for ever, passionately, for ever, I love you, I love you, *si amatissimo amante.*"

The *sbell' idol mio*, as Paulette called him, was rapidly becoming a fallen idol in the political world of the Convention. Paulette knew this, but the knowledge only increased her determination and her misery at the persecution Fréron and she were suffering. Finally, late in October 1797, profiting by a brief respite in the campaign in Italy, Napoleon intervened decisively in his sister's affairs and she submitted. It fell to Lucien to write to his friend Fréron that his letters to Paulette would no longer be delivered to her.

This was the end of Pauline Bonaparte's first serious romance. It was certainly serious, as is shown by its duration and the tenacity of Pauline in the face of family opposition. The letters, doubtless dashed off, certainly not written for a history of which she had no expectation, reflect maturity of sentiment for all the copy-book phraseology. No doubt she wanted marriage, because marriage, especially to a man of importance, seemed to her the natural step for her to take; hence in part the tenacity. But when she knew Fréron to be discredited, she wanted even more to marry him. This shows her instincts of loyalty. She was not deterred by the disclosure of his private life. Her emotions were fully engaged, and expressed with utter sincerity.

Pauline Bonaparte as a girl by Jeanne Maudhuit. This portrait, lent
by the Bowes Museum, Barnard Castle, now hangs in
the British Embassy in Paris

Photo Mansell Collection

General Victor
Emmanuel Leclerc,
first husband of
Pauline Bonaparte

Photo Giraudon

Toussaint Louverture,
leader of the Negro
rebellion in
San Domingo

Photo Giraudon

3. Marriage
1797

THE FAMILY, FOR ALL THEIR RELIEF AT THE OUTCOME OF "the business of Paulette", recognised that she was marriageable and that there would be no peace till she was married. But the first thing was to give her a change of scene, and where better than Italy, where Napoleon was established in vice-regal state after his series of brilliant successes against the Austrians. On February 2, 1797, the Austrians had surrendered the great fortress town of Mantua and northern Italy was virtually in French hands. Napoleon had sent for his family, and, preceded by Joseph and Louis, Signora Letizia arrived at Milan with her brother, the Abbé Fesch, and Paulette and Caroline. Paulette did not meet Napoleon till later in February, in Bologna, and though nothing is recorded of this interview, she appears to have repressed the resentment she felt for the part he had played in preventing the marriage to Fréron. Towards Joséphine her feelings were very different.

She had never till then met Joséphine, who received the two young ladies and their mother with all the charm and grace for which she was famous. Nevertheless, all the Bonapartes disliked Joséphine. They were Corsican, she was French, yet not the kind of Frenchwoman to whom they had become accustomed; a West Indian planter's daughter, a Créole, with indolent, secret ways. They suspected that Napoleon had married her because she was the widow of an aristocrat. They were determined to show that they were better than she was. They were sure she was not good enough for Napoleon.

Paulette shared these prejudices, but her instinctive dislike ran deeper. She recognised Joséphine at first sight as a *femme-*

femme, a woman, all woman, who had captured her brother and would know how to hold him by her femininity. Had she been a little chit of a girl, Paulette could have made friends with Napoleon's wife. She would have liked to see Napoleon suitably married. But not to this exotic mysterious woman in whom she instinctively saw a rival and an adversary, perhaps because she knew that, like herself, Joséphine had a peculiar power over men. It was the antipathy which one very feminine woman sometimes feels for another.

The general family prejudice, her deep instincts, and her resentment at Joséphine's interference in her own private life, all combined to set Paulette against her at first sight. On the occasion of this first meeting, as soon as Joséphine's back was turned, she put out her tongue. As Joséphine's fortunes rose with Napoleon's, she found more effective ways of expressing her dislike: Paulette's deepening aversion to her sister-in-law was a factor in Joséphine's eventual repudiation by Napoleon.

Paulette was enchanted by her new life, by the semi-royal grandeur which surrounded the General's family, by the theatre and all the distractions of a great city, and as spring came, by excursions and picnics in the countryside. A charming picture of her at this time has been left by the poet and traveller Antoine-Vincent Arnault, then serving on General Bonaparte's staff. "She was at once the prettiest and the most unreasonable person imaginable, with the deportment of a schoolgirl, laughing at nothing and everything, contradicting the most eminent personages, sticking out her tongue at her sister-in-law behind her back, nudging my knee when I wasn't paying her enough attention" [the poet once sat next to her at dinner], "and drawing upon herself from time to time the most terrifying looks of reproof from her brother . . . But all the same a naturally good child though without any principles; someone capable of doing good from pure caprice."

Arnault's rather condescending description of Paulette as "the prettiest person imaginable" certainly does less than justice to her looks. She was slight in figure, graceful in her movements, and as a very young woman, before the sun and fevers of San Domingo left their mark, she had an exquisite complexion. Her features had the characteristic strong Bonaparte bone-structure —firm cheek-bones, a pronounced little chin, a straight nose, a small mouth with Cupid's bow lips, although she had rather large ears, which she preferred to cover. At sixteen these fine contours were moulded by the bloom and smoothness of youth, and the dancing, lustrous eyes gave to the whole a harmony which Laure Permon described as perfect. Napoleon considered her the most beautiful woman of her time. "Beautiful Princess" he called her later in his letters, though endearments were in a minority in their voluminous correspondence, most of which consists of stern and formal rebukes for his sister's latest folly. After making due allowance for fraternal affection, and a certain prejudice because of a family resemblance to the head of the clan, we can agree, on the evidence of her contemporaries and of the many portraits that were made of her, however idealised, that Pauline Bonaparte was a beautiful woman.

In intervals of campaigning Napoleon bestirred himself to find her a suitable husband. His choice lighted on the youthful General Victor Emmanuel Leclerc. Leclerc was the son of a well-to-do mill-owner from Pontoise. Napoleon had always insisted that any husband of his sister's must be well-endowed with worldly goods. Leclerc, moreover, was so devoted to Napoleon that he cultivated his mannerisms, his gestures and his facial expressions.

There is no doubt that this match was arranged, though there were later the usual scandalous stories; it was suggested that Napoleon hurriedly contrived it on learning that the two were lovers. Paulette was delighted when the proposition was put to her. She immediately accepted this grave, polite young man of twenty-six; or it may be that she would have been delighted to marry anybody. Her "little Leclerc" as she called him (he was a small, neat man) seemed to her a perfectly adequate husband. The marriage took place on June 14, 1797, at the château of Monbello near Verona which Napoleon had taken over for his family. Paulette was nearly seventeen. It was wonderful to be alive, young, married, spoilt and fêted. In July Napoleon moved his headquarters back to Milan. General and Madame Leclerc naturally went too. The château of Monbello had been splendid, but nothing compared to Milan, with its sophisticated society, its balls and theatres, the daily fashion parade along the Corso. The Signora left for Ajaccio to repair the family mansion, taking with her Elisa and her Corsican husband, Bacciochi, who, already legally married in Marseille in May, had profited by Paulette's wedding to have their own union blessed by the church. Paulette was thus, after Joséphine, the leading lady in Milan.

Apart from what she had learnt in provincial Marseille and during her earlier short stay in Milan, Paulette knew little about the world of society. What more natural than that she should turn for advice to her husband's aide-de-camp, young Captain Hippolyte Charles. A Parisian, he had all the fashionable graces —he was a good talker, a good dancer, a ladies' man. Madame Leclerc was seen about with him everywhere, and tongues wagged. Paulette may have been imprudent, but nothing more. She was at this and for some time to come in love after her fashion with her "little Leclerc". Any incipient flirtation was in any case abruptly ended when she heard that the gallant Captain was Joséphine's beau. In a fury of indignation she alerted Napoleon. He cashiered Charles from the army and forbade him to set foot in Milan. There was a terrible scene with Joséphine, but—not for the last time—Napoleon forgave her. She herself protected Charles, continued to see him over the years, and in fact was instrumental in helping him to make a considerable fortune in civil life as supplier to the army.

Fouché, the Vicar-of-Bray Minister and police chief who served successive French régimes, called the Leclerc match a "garrison marriage" and alleged that it went wrong from the beginning. Fouché's evidence on the Bonaparte family is tainted —towards the end of the Empire he became with Talleyrand Napoleon's bitterest and most insidious opponent—and his memoirs are full of prejudice. Arnault, the poet, is once again a much more reliable witness. Describing a visit to Leclerc, he says that he found him at home with his wife "intoxicated by his happiness, in love and full of ambition. His wife struck me as very happy too, not only to be married to him, but also to be married at all." That describes Paulette's feelings towards Leclerc very accurately.

On October 17 the victorious end of the campaign against Austria was registered in the Treaty of Campo Formio. France was strengthened by obtaining the Rhine as frontier, Austria weakened by the subtraction of most of Northern Italy from her rule and the creation of the republics of Genoa, Lombardy, Modena and Bologna. General Bonaparte's work in Italy was brilliantly accomplished, and he was free to return to the central battlefield, Paris, the field where the political struggle would be fought out. The years of revolution had denuded France of able civil administrators and disrupted the civil service. The victorious army led by Napoleon had become the prop of the Republic, the generals under his command were the ablest administrators available. Napoleon was well aware of the position he had acquired and the opportunities that lay to hand.

4. Motherhood
1798-9

PARIS! PAULETTE ASSUMED THAT SHE AND LECLERC would accompany Napoleon to the city of her dreams, but she had to restrain her impatience for a few months. Leclerc was ordered to stay behind in Milan with his brigade. Paulette meanwhile discovered that she was pregnant. The following spring (April 20, 1798) she gave birth to a boy. Brought up, like all the Bonapartes, to admire the romantic story of Ossian, she named him Dermid (adding for good family measure the names Louis-Napoleon). Most cultivated Frenchmen at this period would have recognised this outlandish name as that of one of the heroes of the legendary third-century Celtic bard who had been made fashionable by the Scotsman James Macpherson's reconstruction in the late eighteenth century. Napoleon took Ossian-Macpherson with him in his travelling library, and literary figures like Lamartine, Chateaubriand and Madame de Staël were equal enthusiasts. Paulette, in choosing this name for her son, was thoroughly in the romantic movement of the day.

Napoleon, the man of the moment, judged that the time had not come for a bid for power. The pear, as he said, was not ripe. Fresh military laurels would be his most useful asset. After an inspection at the Channel ports, he rejected the idea of an invasion of England. A blow at England through India was more attractive. It appealed to Napoleon's vague vision of himself as the new Alexander the Great. It appealed to the politicians of the Directory, at grips with a financial crisis, as a means of crippling English commercial supremacy and distracting a volatile public from grievances at home.

The birth of Dermid was followed by post-natal complications which probably played their part in the disorders, both physical and psychological, which overtook Paulette during her brief existence. As soon as she had sufficiently recovered, she went to Florence. There she learnt that on May 19 Napoleon had sailed for Egypt at the head of an expeditionary force. In July she arrived at last in Paris, with Leclerc who had been appointed Commanding General of the Army of England, which had been massed in Brittany to distract British attention from the Egyptian expedition. The Leclercs settled down in the rue de la Victoire, two steps from Joséphine's house.

Paulette plunged with zest and abandon into the social round of the city—the theatre, the Italian Opera, the ballet, the "Folies" of the day, the drive up the Champs-Elysées to Bagatelle, the charming private park in the Bois de Boulogne taken over by Napoleon from the former royal family. Acquired by Lord Hertford during the Restoration, it was sold by Sir Richard Wallace to the City of Paris in 1905.

And of course there were dinners and balls in private houses. There she met her own family and intimates, prominent men in the revolutionary government and their wives, and Napoleon's military colleagues. This was a new society, already beginning to centre on the Bonaparte family—the prelude to the era of the Consulate. Laure Permon thought it vulgar and contrasted the times unfavourably with the style and elegance of the epoch of Louis XVI, about which her mother never ceased talking. Then every fashionable lady had a bath-tub and never let two days go by without bathing. Apartments were expected to be very cool and fragrant with flowers in summer, very close and warm in winter. Now, since the Revolution, "the French people, in becoming fraternized, ceased to have clean hands. They no longer liked good things: soft, capacious easy chairs, thick carpets, down pillows, all the refinements of the culinary art." In other words, the *style Louis XVI* was out of fashion.

The Bonapartes were soon to introduce their own personal revolution in taste. The styles of furniture, furnishing and clothes lacked the elegance and comfort which had reached such a high pitch in the reigns of Louis XV and Louis XVI, but had their own severe and magnificent *ligne*. Much of it was inspired by Napoleon's exploits in Egypt. Sphinxes and sirens, obelisks and pyramids blended with recollections of Roman, particularly Pompeian, art, brought a note of Oriental fantasy to the classical styles of the Consulate and Empire. When Paulette had a great house of her own, she entirely redecorated it in the new style. And as to Laure Permon's complaint that people seemed nowadays to prefer to go dirty, this was certainly not true of the Bonapartes, who were all addicted to bathing and installed splendid bathrooms in their palaces and châteaux.

The Permons lived very near the rue de la Victoire and in their fine hôtel received a great deal under the Directory. Laure Permon, her pen dipped in envy, recorded her impression of the effect Paulette had on this select and narrow Parisian society of the Directory era. The occasion was a ball at the house of Laure's mother, Signora Letizia's friend. Paulette had taken infinite pains over her dress, which was on classical lines in imitation of a Bacchante, the material of fine India muslin, with a pattern of grapes and vine-leaves and a deep bordering of gold. Over the dress, pinned to her shoulders by classical cameos, she wore a tunic in the Greek style. The dress was fastened tightly by a gold band below the bosom. As she entered the ball-room there was a buzz of admiration from the men, who thronged round the dazzling creature. "The ladies were all much piqued at the beauty and elegant dress of Madame Leclerc. They whispered to one another, but loud enough to be heard by Paulette, that such an impudent display of extravagance was exceedingly unbecoming in a woman who had been almost starving only three years before." To the end, Pauline was envied and criticized in the social world of Paris.

Leclerc was often away from the rue de la Victoire, at his headquarters at Rennes attending to his troops in Brittany. Paulette, who could never be for long without a cavalier, found one in the middle-aged, worldly General Beurnonville, whom she called "her Ajax". Once again it is Laure Permon who has left to posterity an account of Paulette's friendship with Beurnonville and two prominent younger generals of the day—Macdonald and Moreau. An intangible aura of scandal hangs about Laure's account. But she was prejudiced against her childhood friend, through jealousy or through her feeling that Paulette was an embarrassment to Napoleon, for whom she had an uncritical admiration. There is no reason to suppose that the youthful Madame Leclerc went very far with these men, though she certainly went beyond the bounds of discretion. Paulette liked men, and could not live without men constantly and familiarly around her. But the story of the three generals does not sound like a serious and complicated triangular love-affair, as it was represented in some contemporary memoirs. Paulette's interest, apart from her absolute need for masculine companionship, was instinctively to learn more of the world and its ways from these three men, each of whom was experienced and knowledgeable. Paulette may have been flirtatious: she was also a Bonaparte, quick and eager to learn and to better herself.

The spectacle of young Madame Leclerc driving this *troika* of generals in her husband's absence was widely commented on. Madame de Staël observed that it was natural that she should not wish to separate from a demi-god, referring to Paulette's pet-name for General Beurnonville. It was evidently time to halt. But she could not bring herself to dismiss the three generals. She would have quite liked to be left with one cavalier, preferably Macdonald. So she tried to poison his mind against the other two. The three men, who were friends, compared notes and of their own accord decided to make the break. "Ajax", as the senior, was deputed to deliver formal letters from the other two. After this humiliating experience Paulette never repeated the experiment of keeping three men dancing attendance on her at once.

Unknown to Paulette, events were shaping themselves in a way which was to lead Napoleon at a stroke to a position of supreme power and transform the fortunes of his family. The invasion of Egypt was proceeding favourably when the destruction of the French fleet by Nelson at Aboukir on August 1,

1798, left Napoleon and the invading force cut off from supplies and the outside world. Undeterred by this disaster, Napoleon, with unshaken self-reliance, crushed the Mameluks at the Battle of the Pyramids and proceeded to use the resources of Egypt to maintain the expeditionary force. After the French had overrun Palestine, the Turks belatedly made an effort, in the summer of 1799, to eject them from Egypt, and landed ten thousand men at Aboukir. Napoleon destroyed the Turkish force on July 26. His instinct now told him that this was the moment for him to return to Paris. The morale of the French army was high, the Egyptians had been beaten into subjection, the Turks had failed in the effort to save the province. Leaving Kléber in command, he sailed secretly from Alexandria on August 23, 1799, in a small frigate, with Murat, Berthier and a few others, and, after several narrow escapes from the English patrols, landed at Fréjus on October 9.

Leclerc at this time was at Lyons, having been given a new mission: the reorganisation of the Army of Italy. The Treaty of Campo Formio had become a dead letter, Austria and Russia had united to eject the French from northern Italy, and during the spring of 1799, while Napoleon was conquering Palestine and Syria, the French had suffered several defeats at Austrian and Russian hands. Alarm was great in Paris. The country was on the verge of bankruptcy. Politicians and ordinary citizens alike felt that only Napoleon could save the Republic.

By coincidence Lucien and Joseph happened to be with Leclerc at Lyons when the news that Napoleon had landed in the south of France was received in that city. All three men proceeded to meet him. Paulette was not with her husband. Nor did Joséphine succeed in meeting Napoleon en route: she set out from Paris by another road and missed him. Joséphine had every reason to hasten to reassure her husband, since it was common knowledge that during his absence she had again taken Hippolyte Charles as her lover. The missed rendez-vous was a misfortune for Joséphine, which the Bonapartes were able to exploit in their campaign to persuade their brother to repudiate

42

her. A contemporary records that he had never seen such hatred as that which Paulette showed towards her sister-in-law when, on his return to Paris, the family went round to Napoleon's house to offer good wishes on his safe return. Though scarcely a model of fidelity herself, she could not forgive Joséphine's disloyalty to Napoleon.

Three weeks later Paulette was at the Théâtre Feydeau with her mother, Madame Permon and Caroline. All were anxious, as they knew that Napoleon and Lucien were deeply involved in the political manœuvrings to change the constitution and place Napoleon at the head of affairs. It was the evening of the 19th of Brumaire (November 10, 1799). The day before, the Council of Ancients, on the motion of one of the conspirators, had decreed that the two other major councils, the Upper and the Lower House, should sit at the Château of St. Cloud, the former royal palace on the further bank of the Seine just beyond the Bois de Boulogne, and that General Bonaparte should assume command of all troops in the Paris region. In the theatre news was anxiously awaited of events at St. Cloud.

During the interval one of the actors advanced to the front of the stage and announced that revolution had broken out at St. Cloud. "General Bonaparte has only just escaped assassination by traitors to the fatherland." There was a cry from Paulette, whose shoulders shook convulsively. The Signora paled, but spoke sharply to her daughter. "Have you not heard that nothing happened to your brother? Be quiet, get up, we must leave at once and get news."

With her daughters and Madame Permon, the Signora hurried to the Bonaparte house, pushing through the crowds of civilians and soldiers who blocked the rue de la Victoire. There they learnt that, after a moment of peril at which Napoleon had for once lost his nerve and Lucien had saved the day, the *coup d'état* had succeeded. A Directory of three had been proclaimed, consisting of Sieyès, Roger Ducos and, with the title of First Consul, General Bonaparte. "There is a pike," remarked Madame Permon, "who will gobble up the other two fish."

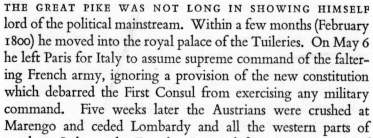

5

"Why didst thou promise such a
beauteous day,
And make me travel forth without my cloak?"

1800-1

THE GREAT PIKE WAS NOT LONG IN SHOWING HIMSELF
lord of the political mainstream. Within a few months (February
1800) he moved into the royal palace of the Tuileries. On May 6
he left Paris for Italy to assume supreme command of the falter-
ing French army, ignoring a provision of the new constitution
which debarred the First Consul from exercising any military
command. Five weeks later the Austrians were crushed at
Marengo and ceded Lombardy and all the western parts of
northern Italy to the French. It was left to Moreau, one of
Paulette's three military friends, to complete the Austrian defeat
at Hohenlinden at the end of the year. The Austrians finally
gave up the struggle and concluded peace the following February
at Lunéville.

Napoleon said to his secretary, Bourrienne, on taking up
quarters in the Tuileries, that the important thing was not to
go and live in the Tuileries but to stay there. After his return
in triumph that summer from the victorious Italian campaign
it soon became apparent that many Frenchmen were determined
that his tenure of supreme power should be abruptly shortened.
Throughout the Consulate Napoleon's life was in danger from
extremists in two camps, Jacobin and Royalist. Even in his own
family circle he was criticized for betraying the principles of the
Revolution and concentrating too much power in the hands of
one man. Lucien, his junior by six years, a patriotic and ardent

44

republican, felt that his brother was betraying him and the Republic. His behaviour after Marengo, his court at the Tuileries, convinced the passionate and brilliant young man that he and his brother would never see eye to eye. He was relieved of his portfolio as Minister of the Interior and went to Spain as Ambassador.

Laure Permon has recorded a scene at the Opéra (where so many of the dramatic moments of the Directory and Consulate were caught for history) after an attempt on the First Consul's life. General Junot, soon to be her husband, had wind of the conspiracy and had tried to dissuade Madame Permon from going to the theatre that evening. But Madame Permon insisted, and the party took their seats punctually at eight o'clock. The boxes were filled. The First Consul was late. At last he appeared in his box, accompanied by Junot and others, and was received with an ovation. As Napoleon was getting up to leave at the end of the performance and buttoning his grey greatcoat over his Guards uniform, Junot rushed round to the Permons' box and whispered, "He has narrowly escaped death, the assassins have just been arrested!"

While Lucien went into virtual exile in Madrid, the rest of the Bonaparte family set themselves up in Paris in style, basking in the radiance of the First Consul. Paulette continued to live in the rue de la Victoire, mostly alone, since Leclerc was away campaigning first with General Moreau in Germany and later on an expedition to Portugal which he led through Spain. Paulette joined him at Bordeaux in the spring of 1801, returning to Paris when he set off for the Spanish border. During the summer she spent much of her time with Joseph at Mortefontaine, and bought a new house in Paris, 38 rue de Courcelles, not far from her future house in the rue du Faubourg St. Honoré.

The Parisian fashions of the Consulate fascinated her. The classical style, inspired by the form-fitting light draperies of Greek statuettes, suited her to perfection. She felt herself, with justice, to be a modern Tanagra figurine, petite and slim. She adored the new English material, a very fine transparent muslin called cambric. Her reputation has suffered from the reproach that she took pleasure in sartorial revelation beyond the bounds of decorum: in fact, as in most affairs of life, she followed the vogue with uninhibited enthusiasm. The abandoned *négligé* of the Consulate was not a creation of Paulette's but a reaction to the squalor of the Revolution and the elegant extravagances of the Monarchy.

There was as yet no formal ceremonial at the Tuileries, though Laure Permon's mother complained that Napoleon, in his first year as First Consul, "affected the little king". According to Laure Permon, who was sixteen in 1800, the family circle at the Tuileries had no more formality than that of any very rich man. Joséphine at this early stage had not even ladies-in-waiting. After her marriage to Junot in that same year Napoleon told Laure Permon: "My intention is to draw round me a numerous family, consisting of my generals and their young wives." Paulette, naturally, was a member of this closed circle, in which, apart from Napoleon's intimates, she can have met few outsiders except the small diplomatic corps of the day. (There were ten Ambassadors and a Swiss Minister.)

Etiquette was even more relaxed at Malmaison, the charming château near Versailles where Joséphine passed the greater part of her time. Napoleon liked Malmaison and insisted on informality. Once a week during this lull in military activity there was a dinner party, in fine weather held out of doors in the park of the château. After dinner the company played cards or, if fine, they played an outdoor game called "barriers", a kind of "prisoners base", and Napoleon would take his coat off and "run like a hare". According to Laure Permon, who joined in these games, Napoleon cheated at cards and broke the rules at "barriers". But, she added indulgently, "these tricks were only calculated to raise a laugh."

Pauline cannot much have enjoyed these parties as an unwilling guest of Joséphine. She preferred to visit Joseph and Julie, the former Mademoiselle Clary of Marseille days, at Mortefontaine. And of course she had her own new fine house in the rue de Courcelles, where she could see whom she liked. Her rather aimless existence at this time and Leclerc's career, relatively undistinguished for a member of Napoleon's family circle, were suddenly transformed by orders which reached Leclerc in mid-October 1801 at his headquarters near Valladolid. He was to return immediately to Paris. There he learnt that he was at last to be a commander-in-chief, leader of an expedition to San Domingo, the large West Indian island which today contains the states of Haiti and the Dominican Republic. This important French possession in the West Indies had been taken over by the negroes under their negro leader, Toussaint Louverture. Napoleon decided on a determined effort to restore French rule.

The recapture of San Domingo, in Napoleon's mind, was to be the spearhead of the restoration of the French position in the Americas. The main objective was not San Domingo but Louisiana, the vast, vaguely delimited area, extending up the Mississippi and Ohio rivers from the Gulf of Mexico to the Great Lakes, which the French had forfeited, with Canada and the rest of their American possessions, after Wolfe defeated Montcalm at Quebec in 1759. Under the peace settlement of 1763 Spain had acquired Louisiana in return for concessions in Europe. After the French Revolution, and before Napoleon came to power, the French Government had tried but failed to persuade the Spaniards to yield up this territory (though they succeeded in obtaining the cession of the Spanish half of San Domingo, the whole of which was thus now a French possession). In the summer of 1800 the First Consul returned to the charge, offering the Spanish royal house Tuscany in return for Louisiana. But the Spanish Government rejected the offer.

Napoleon therefore decided as a first step to restore French rule in the great Caribbean island to which nobody could dispute his claim. He chose his moment with care. By October 1801 the negotiations for peace with England, a necessary preliminary to the restoration of the French Colonial Empire, were well under way. Prospects for a forward policy in the Near East and beyond that against the British position in India were not good, since what was left of the French army had been ejected from Egypt and the British had occupied the country. Laying aside his ambitions in the Orient for the moment, Napoleon concentrated on the Americas.

It was the French Revolution which had lost San Domingo for the French. The Revolutionary proclamation of equality between blacks and whites had led to a terrible slaves' revolt. Toussaint Louverture, a modern Spartacus, had led the revolt and prevailed over the planters and the administration. This then was Leclerc's task—to restore the rule of the central government of France.

Napoleon strongly urged Paulette to go with her husband to San Domingo. Some of her contemporaries asserted that Leclerc's appointment was due to Napoleon's determination to remove Paulette to a good distance from Paris and the actor Lafon, with whom, according to these memorialists, she had been having an affair. Napoleon could not countenance light behaviour in his sister when he was insisting on a strict code of morality in the new society of which he was the head.

Lafon—his name in private life was Pierre Rapenouille—had taken Paris audiences by storm when he made his début as an actor in tragic rôles at the Théâtre Français on September 5, 1800. He was a particular favourite with women theatre-goers, who adored his rendering of the highly romantic heroes of tragedy like the Cid or Bayard. He was supposed to be irresistible to women. There is no reliable evidence that Paulette was one of his conquests or even of his acquaintances. She may well have fallen out of love with Leclerc, whom she rarely saw; she was probably bored; but she had not as yet taken the plunge into promiscuity. Neither of them seems to have found it easy to decide whether she should go to San Domingo. To believe her friend Laure Permon (by now Madame Junot), Leclerc "would willingly have dispensed with this addition to his baggage, for it was a positive calamity after the first quarter of an hour's interview had exhausted the pleasure of surveying the

Letizia Bonaparte,
mother of Napoleon
and Pauline,
by Bertolini

Photo Bulloz

Cardinal Fesch,
Letizia's half-brother,
by Pasqualini

Photo Giraudon

Pauline Bonaparte by Lefèvre, 1806

Photo Giraudon

really beautiful person, to have the burden of amusing, occupying, and taking care of Madame Leclerc."

Paulette herself, while in public professing herself delighted to accompany her husband, was miserable at the prospect of leaving Paris for the West Indies with its reputation for savagery and disease.

"Ah, Laurette," she wailed, "how fortunate you are. You stay in Paris . . . How can my brother be so hard-hearted, so wicked, as to send me into exile among savages and snakes?"

Laurette knew her friend and did not take these demonstrations very seriously. She knew what appealed to Paulette and suggested that she would look very well in Créole costume.

"You really think, Laurette," she enquired, "that I shall look pretty—prettier than usual—in a Créole turban, a short waist and a petticoat of striped muslin?"

Young Madame Junot straightway contrived from scarves and bandanas a passable imitation of the exotic costume of those parts. Paulette dressed herself in them, looked at herself in the glass, and was enchanted. She was so grateful to her young friend that she begged her to come to San Domingo too. Laurette was horrified by the prospect and greatly relieved when her husband happened at that moment to come into the room. Junot, too, was at first alarmed, and asked Paulette in all seriousness whether she had mentioned the idea to Napoleon. The conversation ended with Paulette once again in tears and the Junots considering the whole idea a typical caprice of Paulette's. Yet Junot thought it prudent to tell the First Consul the same day what Paulette had been suggesting. Napoleon, after keeping him in suspense for three days, solemnly told Junot that he was sorry but he could not spare him to go to San Domingo.

Consoling herself with a vast outfit of new dresses, hats and materials, Paulette finally made up her mind and, taking the three-year-old Dermid with her, dolefully left Paris for Brest. It was the beginning of the harshest experience of her life and it remains difficult to understand why Napoleon should have condemned his sister to it, the more so since Leclerc was hardly the man to deal successfully with the situation. His farewell instructions to Leclerc contained a word for Paulette: "Do not forget to give me news of Madame Leclerc; I like to think that she will have some little share in your glory." Paulette laughed wryly when her husband gave her the message. How characteristic of Napoleon! As if glory was what one really cared about. And yet . . . perhaps it was rather splendid to conquer and rule. In any case she would certainly show Napoleon, and France, that she knew how to be a governor's wife.

6. Rendez-vous dans la chambre mortuaire
1802

ON DECEMBER 14, 1801, IN BITTER WINTER WEATHER, THE squadron weighed anchor, thirty-two ships of the line carrying more than 20,000 officers and marines, as well as military doctors and a host of administrators and clerks. Despite the evil reputation of the West Indies, with its notoriously high death rate, and the particular dangers of the present enterprise, morale was high in the fleet. After waiting for twelve days in the Canaries for a squadron from Rochefort which failed to make the rendez-vous, leaving Leclerc short of troops, they moved into warmer waters and life on board the flagship, the *Océan*, became positively gay. Paulette, all her life at her happiest when the centre of an admiring throng of young officers, held her little court on the quarter-deck "in all the radiance of her beauty", as a member of the expedition recorded, "like a living statue recalling the Galatea of the ancients, a marine Venus". Paulette, no doubt, was dressed *à l'Athénienne* the classical style fashionable at the outset of the Consulate. Sometimes she would have the little Dermid brought up on deck and play with him. Affectionate mother and gracious wife of the commander-in-chief, the twenty-one-year-old Paulette had forgotten her infatuation for Fréron, and may not even have been aware that he was aboard another ship of the flotilla. He had had the grace to have himself transferred when he learnt at Brest that he was to sail in the *Océan*. The wretched man who had so disturbed Paulette's adolescent fancies had married his lady of the theatre and was now seeking to remedy his fortunes in this desperate expedition to the Antilles. Within a few weeks of landing he was to be dead of yellow fever.

The squadron made landfall on February 4, 1802, off Cap

Haïtien—Cap Français or Cap de la République, or more familiarly "le Cap", the administrative centre of the colony. The Cape was in the hands of a hostile negro chief, Christophe, and Leclerc was obliged to land his men, horses and equipment as best he could a few miles down the coast. Advancing on Cap Haïtien, he found that Christophe had withdrawn, leaving the town in flames. Barely a hundred colonial houses were habitable, but one of them served well enough for the Commanding General's headquarters. Here he installed Madame Leclerc, with their infant son. Leclerc then set out with determination after the chief rebel. On March 25 he brought Toussaint Louverture to battle. A fortnight later he captured him, and sent him in chains to France. The rebellion to all appearances was quashed, Paulette went out to meet the returning army, welcomed with cries of joy "*mon joli gamin*", as she called Leclerc. The news was received with enthusiasm in Paris, and Napoleon wrote to Leclerc congratulating him warmly and promising handsome rewards on his return to France. This letter, owing to the time required for news to travel between France and the Antilles, did not reach Leclerc till midsummer, by which time events had taken on a very different complexion.

By the time that Leclerc's report was received in Paris seven or eight weeks after the event, peace was about to be concluded with England. With the Peace of Amiens signed on May 27, 1802, and San Domingo, as he thought, safely in French hands, Napoleon felt free to act. He ordered a force to be prepared, ostensibly for the reinforcement of Leclerc but really for a descent on New Orleans. At the same time pressure was revived on the Spaniards to cede Louisiana.

For Paulette this spring-time in the West Indies was an idyll, while fever and disease lurked in the swamps and native settlements, waiting to be called forth by the heat of summer to strike the white man down. The warm but not torrid weather, the romantic scenery of the steep Haitian mountains covered with lush and vivid vegetation, the exotic appearance and clothes of the natives, the fact that she was the reigning queen of the island and the centre of all attentions provided her with exactly the milieu she adored. She kept a collection of tropical plants and a menagerie. She sent the family and friends pots of conserves made from the local fruits, and bottles of liqueurs. She held receptions, dinners and balls at Government House.

But soon the heat, humid and oppressive, became unbearable. The insalubrious conditions in the half-ruined town of Cap Haïtien gave rise to unfamiliar tropical diseases. It may have been at this time that Paulette broke out into the sores of which she still bore the scars when she returned to Paris the following year. She felt ill and listless. In her mirror she saw with dismay that her features had lost their bloom and were becoming lined and yellowed. She was panic-stricken at the thought of Dermid contracting some unknown disease. Medical supplies were running short. There was only one thing to do.

Leclerc decided to move his headquarters and family to the island of La Tortue off the town of Cap Haïtien, where the heat was more supportable and the conditions more hygienic. A strong military guard and a number of civilian administrators accompanied the Leclercs. Paulette's arrival created a sensation among the negroes working on the island. She consented to attend one of their traditional dances, and the member of Leclerc's staff who recorded the bizarre scene was shocked that the General's wife should have been present at this orgiastic display and witnessed such unnamed indecencies.

In later years the scandalmongers like Lewis Goldsmith excelled themselves in besmirching Paulette's reputation during her stay in San Domingo. She was accused of having lovers among members of her husband's staff and even of consorting, for comparison's sake, with negroes. One of Louis XVIII's agents alleged that two of Leclerc's principal generals were her lovers. Leclerc's order threatening with extradition to France white women, "whatever their rank", who consorted with negroes, was held by some to have been aimed at his wife.

The picture we have from other sources is very different. We hear of Paulette visiting soldiers ill in hospital or taking a glass of wine with the garrison. We know that, at Turtle Island as at Cap Haïtien, she held a regular salon—a court it might have seemed to her, with dancing and music. All decorous, as became the wife of the commander, and a little fantastic, as became the exotic island: the members of her personal staff wore a uniform of her own designing—a kind of hussar's tunic with yellow pantaloons and striped stockings in the style of Egyptian Mameluks, capped by a plumed helmet.

All the stories, however, cannot be dismissed as hostile anti-Bonaparte propaganda. For example, Norvins, Leclerc's secretary, a man not prejudiced against his master or his wife, hints at indiscretions by Paulette. And it does seem that there is something in the theory of some contemporary writers that the violent surroundings and the demoralising climate of Haiti were not without their effect on Paulette's character. There can at all events be little doubt that the intolerable experience of Haiti, with its macabre amalgam of horror and over-excitement, was a turning-point in her life. Paulette was not made for the horrible or the tragic. She was the essence of frivolity and lightheartedness. Everything about her was superficial—her capriciousness, her eagerness for the tinsel and finery of life, her love of the salon and the chandelier—except for a hard Bonaparte core which came out in rare moments of loyalty to her brother and a sense of the greatness of France. It was not her fault that circumstances had cast her for a rôle of majesty she was incapable of fulfilling and thrown her into a dramatic current of history which she generally preferred to ignore. The last terrible months in San Domingo showed that she possessed qualities other than capriciousness and superficiality.

The summer brought with it not only the great heat but an epidemic of yellow fever, which rapidly decimated the French occupation forces, military and civilian. The negroes took heart and, led by Christophe, girded themselves to exterminate the rapidly diminishing French army. The brigades of loyal negroes which the French had formed deserted early in September. Leclerc left Turtle Island and returned to Cap Haïtien to rally his discouraged and diminishing forces. His wife insisted on going with him. In Cap Haïtien there were no longer any medical supplies: Paulette, heedless of the risk, visited the sick soldiers in the appalling conditions of the hospitals where they were dying in shoals of the fever. At the Commander-in-Chief's house she made valiant efforts to keep up appearances. Receptions and concerts took place as usual. The orchestra still played, and if an instrumentalist suddenly fell out, a victim to yellow fever, those that remained played on, still wearing the quaint uniform Paulette had designed for them. These receptions at the General's house were known as the *"rendez-vous dans la chambre mortuaire"*. But everyone respected the courage of the young woman who insisted on holding them.

Leclerc urged his wife to leave the doomed island. Paulette refused to flee, though at one moment she offered to comply if Leclerc would give her enough money to maintain herself in style in Paris. Characteristically, for she usually thought in terms of personalities, she wanted to be sure of being as well dressed and of having as splendid a carriage as her sister Caroline, recently married to Murat. But Paulette probably never seriously intended to leave. "My sister Murat is simply an ordinary bourgeois wife," she concluded. "All the bourgeois have carriages. Here I reign like Joséphine. I am the first lady."

Fifteen hundred officers, twelve thousand soldiers and marines, two thousand civilians, had died of yellow fever. The French position seemed desperate. With his two thousand troops, all the effective fighting men that remained, Leclerc determined to make a final attempt to crush the insurgents. Before the attack he instructed his private secretary to put Paulette and Dermid on board one of the ships in the harbour if he received word that the attempt had failed. Paulette refused to move. "You can quit, all of you. You are not Bonaparte's sister." The sound of cannon and rifle fire showed that the battle was engaged. After a short time the half-expected message came. Norvins, thinking all was over, told Paulette she must leave instantly for the ship. She refused, and had to be carried down to the port forcibly by the four troopers Leclerc had left behind. As one of the troopers carried her and another carried Dermid, she smiled at the little boy who was fingering the plumes of the trooper's helmet. She laughed outright at the incongruous appearance of her attendants, some of whom carried a parasol in one hand and a drawn sabre in the other. "Look," she said to Norvins, "we look like a masked ball at the opera!" At the last moment an aide-de-camp rushed up to announce that the rebels were routed.

A few weeks later Leclerc fell victim to the dreaded fever, and in ten days was dead. There was nothing left but evacuation. It was the end. Before the coffin was closed, in a passion of grief, and recalling the ancient custom of bereavement in Corsica, she cut off her hair and strewed it over her husband's features. A week later, on November 8, 1802, with Dermid, she sailed from the terrible island for home, bearing the embalmed body with her, and in a separate leaden casket encased in gold, the heart of her "*joli gamin*". Twenty-two, a widow, shaken and ill, pallid and shorn, all she had left was Dermid, miraculously unscathed by the yellow fever or a native knife. She was grateful to her husband whom she had never deeply loved for the gift of what now seemed the most precious possession in the world.

The death of the Commander-in-Chief and the decimation of the French forces by disease put paid to the attempt to recover San Domingo from the negroes. Napoleon did not learn the full extent of the disaster till the last days of the year. Meanwhile the United States had become thoroughly alarmed when in October 1802 the Spanish officials in New Orleans at French behest closed the lower Mississippi to American shipping. Napoleon understood that his designs on Louisiana must be abandoned and renounced French claims on the territory in return for a payment of sixty million francs. The attempt to restore the French position in the Americas had ended in failure.

II

Spring's honeyed cud

7. Paris

1803

ON DISEMBARKING AT TOULON ON NEW YEAR'S DAY 1803 after an eight weeks' voyage Paulette wrote to Napoleon: "I have arrived at Toulon after an appalling crossing and with my health ruined. This is the last of my sorrows: I have brought back with me the remains of my poor Leclerc. Pity poor Paulette, she is thoroughly miserable."

Even at fifteen, in her letters to Fréron, Paulette had learnt to express herself in the stilted fashion of the day. The style remained with her through life. But behind the mannered language and the theatrical approach, there is an authentic note of misery, the desperate appeal of a young woman who had passed through a horrible experience and felt lost and uncertain. She must have reflected during the miserable weeks of a winter crossing of the Atlantic on the sudden and terrible blows she had suffered, the failure of an enterprise which had started so successfully, so gaily, the squalor and stench of the yellow fever, the desperate days of danger at the end, the wretched death of Leclerc. She could not be sure what the future held in store, what her position would be in Paris, how her stern brother would receive the widow of a commander who had lost France a colony.

Her health had suffered, there was no doubt about that. She was too ill to be present at the Panthéon, where Leclerc was interred with full military honours.

Madame Junot recorded that after her return from San Domingo she was "faded, nay withered". Yet many of her contemporaries, among them Madame de Rémusat and Fouché, opponents both, noted that, despite her undermined health, her beauty was even more brilliant. This febrile quality of beauty was to last Paulette till her death-bed.

She need not have had qualms about the reception that awaited her. Napoleon, who had become Consul for life on August 1, 1802, and was now the undisputed master of France, assigned a pension of 60,000 francs to his widowed sister. With Leclerc's fortune, larger than expected, she was a comparatively rich woman. The affection and conversation of Joseph and Julie, with whom she went to stay at Mortefontaine, helped to restore her shattered morale. She quickly grasped the fact that, as one of the sisters of the First Consul, she enjoyed a high and privileged position in the State. Wealth and position—what could be more congenial. It was not long before she felt able and eager to return to Paris. The First Consul's sister must have a proper establishment and the proper accoutrements. So the first thing she did, in this surge of renewed interest in being Paulette, was to buy a carriage, a gilded carriage, far more magnificent than Madame Murat's. Next she bought a splendid new house in the rue du Faubourg St. Honoré (now the British Embassy) from the heirs of the Duc de Charost who had died six months before, and in April 1803 she moved into the hôtel.

Having observed mourning for six months, she was ready to plunge without restraint into the gay and ebullient society of Paris. Napoleon, taking the view that the death of a brother-in-law of the ruler of France was a matter of national concern, tried to restrain her—without much effect. She was entranced by the pace and brilliance of the great city. Nobody seemed to give a thought to the disastrous San Domingo expedition; what was the loss of a colony? There was prosperity and peace. Everything centred, as usual, on the First Consul and his entourage. It was true, as Madame Junot noted, that "the Oriental luxury which the Emperor afterwards introduced into his Court was not then known". His preference was for plainness and severity. Napoleon was strict in these matters. He himself was always dressed soberly, in severe, plainly-cut dark clothes. Soon after he became First Consul he had been persuaded to have himself fitted for a magnificent highly-decorated evening coat. But he felt uncomfortable and only wore it once. On occasion he could express himself very disagreeably and then leave the room ostentatiously if the ladies at his receptions wore dresses too décolleté for the severe canons of the Consular Court. But the *haute couture* of the day had come to stay. The new vogue was the robe *à la Psyché*, an extension of the prevailing classical style, extremely low-cut, with a full skirt and a train. The young dressmaker J. H. Leroy had inaugurated his reign in fashionable Paris, and the Government itself had given the impulse by actively promoting the revival of trade in the cloth-manu-facturing towns.

France was at peace, since the defeat of Austria at Marengo and the conclusion of the Treaty of Amiens with England on May 27, 1802. English visitors, many of whom had known the France of the *ancien régime* and were intensely curious to see the new France and the extraordinary man at its head, flocked across the Channel. Some made the journey—an arduous one in those times—just for a day in Paris, to see the sights and if possible Bonaparte himself. Others came for longer, mixed freely in Parisian society and met the new rulers of France. Fox came over for some weeks and had several conversations with the First Consul. His final judgment was that he was "a young man intoxicated with success". Fox himself evidently made an impression; years later, at St. Helena, Napoleon recalled his affection for this man of good heart and large, generous views.

Those like the Countess of Bessborough who had known the France of Louis XVI well found things greatly changed but not the less interesting for that. She and her husband were in Paris from mid-December 1802 to the end of February 1803, and as prominent figures in London society immediately gained the entrée into the political and social life of the French capital. Lady Bessborough, now forty-one, had known France well in her youth and had been a friend of Marie Antoinette. She found some old friends like the Noailles and the Luynes. But most of the people she met were the new Napoleonic society, generals like Moreau, Junot, Berthier and Bernadotte, politicians like Talleyrand. These in fact were the people with position, money and influence. They gave brilliant parties, talked endlessly, welcomed the English. If you went to the right places you were bound to find all the leading men, "from the generals to the savants". How different from London! There, even in the best society where Lady Bessborough reckoned she lived, you could meet clever and celebrated men only with the greatest difficulty, as they preferred to keep to themselves. In Paris the clever and celebrated men were always there, ready to talk about everything from themselves to serious matters of state. She was fascinated by Junot's story of his rise in life, which started when Bonaparte suddenly called on him, an unknown sergeant, and dictated him a rapid order on the battlefield. A shell landed near them and covered them and the paper with dust; Junot coolly exclaimed that it would serve as sand to dry the ink.

This was the heady atmosphere of Napoleonic society during the lull of 1802, a military atmosphere in which young conquerors were to the fore. Lady Bessborough confessed that she could not "move without a regiment of generals and *beaux esprits à mes trousses*". When one was tired of receptions there was the opera, where Madame Bonaparte sat in a box "fitted up like the Royal one in London", there was the author of *Les Liaisons Dangereuses*, or Madame de Staël's latest book if one ever had time to read. The most splendid of all parties were those given by the Minister for Foreign Affairs, Talleyrand. She went to a dinner of seventy-eight persons where she was presented by mistake as the English Ambassadress.

Everybody from across the Channel wanted to see Napoleon and many were equally curious to have a look at Joséphine, variously thought of as a martyr or a *femme galante*, according to one's sympathies with her husband. The inrush of distinguished visitors into Paris during the Peace was such that Napoleon organised receptions at the Tuileries, during which the foreign visitors were presented to the First Consul and his lady. Lady Bessborough, to her mortification, was not summoned. After

London, she found the uncertainty about etiquette disconcerting. The French did not seem to know whether to treat the First Consul as a king or not. The truth, of course, was that Napoleon himself had not yet made up his mind to take the final plunge and assume royal or imperial status. The Consular receptions were relatively unceremonial affairs. The ladies to be presented formed a circle, and the First Consul and Joséphine walked round speaking to each in turn. Miss Mary Berry, another English visitor, described Joséphine as being rather under-dressed on these occasions.

The most formidable woman in Paris was undoubtedly the ugly, passionate, fearless Madame de Staël. Daughter of the Swiss financier Jacques Necker, who became Director General of the French Treasury in 1776 when she was ten years old, Germaine at the age of twenty married an attaché at the Swedish Embassy in Paris, Baron de Staël-Holstein. She had just published *Delphine*, re-stating her strongly held views on liberty in love, religion and politics. By temperament and attainment cast for the rôle of Egeria, she had been a passionate enthusiast for Napoleon at the outset of his career. But the modern Numa Pompilius had repulsed her. When she enquired who in his eyes was the most superior of womankind he had replied: "She who has most children."

Since then she had viewed his increasingly authoritarian tendencies with alarm, and in *Delphine* threw down the challenge. She was to fight Napoleon for the rest of his life, and such was the power and penetration of her pen that she was constantly harried by the régime and frequently took refuge abroad. At St. Helena Napoleon said: "After all is said and done, Madame de Staël is a woman of great talent, very distinguished, of very keen intelligence: she has won her place. It might be said that if instead of carping at me, she had taken my side, it would have been useful to me."

Another house where everyone, Parisian and foreign alike, wanted to go was Madame Récamier's. Jeanne Françoise Julie Adélaïde Bernard, daughter of a notary of Lyons, was born in

1777 and at the age of sixteen married a wealthy Paris banker of forty-three, Jacques Récamier, himself a Lyonnais by birth. The relations between the youthful Juliette and her middle-aged husband are something of a mystery; some of Madame Récamier's contemporaries even suggested that she was his natural daughter and that he married her, in the troubled days of the Terror, so as to be able to leave her his fortune if he fell under the guillotine—as he confidently expected to do. However this may be, the ménage was a happy one. The banker's chief enjoyment was to provide his young and beautiful wife with the surroundings which enabled her to become the reigning beauty of Paris.

Little is recorded of Madame Récamier's father except that he was a singularly handsome man. Her mother had intelligence and charm as well as beauty. All these qualities were inherited by Juliette in a marked degree. To the end of her life—she died in 1849—she exercised a rarely rivalled fascination over an innumerable circle of friends drawn from every class of society and of every political hue. In 1802, at the age of twenty-five, she was already the most talked-of woman in Paris. Madame Lenormant, her niece and therefore perhaps a biased judge, described her beautiful throat and shoulders, her small mouth, pearly teeth, naturally curling black hair, her brilliancy of complexion. Yet Madame Junot, a more critical judge of her contemporaries, was also ecstatic about Madame Récamier's beauty and fascination, a woman "whose love has been the object of universal desire, yet whose virtue has remained pure. She was a peculiar and gifted being, formed by nature in one of her most beneficent moods as a perfect model."

Fox was favourably impressed by her. Mary Berry recognised in her "the decided beauty of the *new* world", though she found her way of dressing affected, her manner simpering and pretentious. But Miss Berry was judging the queen of Paris society by the different standards of London. The Napoleonic social world was certainly new, different and brash. Some features of it were so free as to be shocking to a visiting Londoner,

The Empress Joséphine
by Gérard

Photo Bulloz

The Empress Marie
Louise by Gérard

Photo Bulloz

Prince Camillo Borghese, second husband of Pauline Bonaparte,
by Gérard

Photo Brogi-Giraudon

particularly the disconcerting tendency of Parisian hostesses to receive their guests reclining on a day-bed in the lightly-clothed fashion of the day. On her very first day in Paris before Christmas in 1802, Lady Bessborough was electrified to hear that the evening before, at a ball in her house, Madame Récamier had gone to bed in the middle of the party and "let anybody come and look at her". Lady Bessborough, all curiosity, received an invitation to a reception at the banker's house two days later. There, sure enough, was the hostess in bed—"that beautiful bed you saw prints of—muslin and gold curtains, great looking-glasses at the side, incense pots, etc., and muslin sheets trimmed with lace, and beautiful white shoulders exposed perfectly uncovered to view . . . The room was full of men."

No doubt this kind of freedom on social occasions was astonishing to English eyes. But décolletage and form-revealing dresses in the classical style, ushered in by the sense of liberation after the Terror, had come to stay. Napoleon tried to insist on more decorous fashions, at least on ceremonial occasions. But outside the court a good deal of freedom persisted. Paulette was by no means exceptional in her penchant for classical undress. It was the prevailing mode.

Paulette, Joséphine and Juliette Récamier were the most talked-of women in Paris, all beautiful, all fascinating in their own way. They are not to be thought of as social rivals, except for the feline rivalry that existed between Paulette and her sister-in-law. As a social figure Madame Récamier was of course far more accessible than the ladies of the Bonaparte family. She was a social hostess in the true sense of the word. Joséphine was the consort of the head of the State. Paulette could have had a brilliant court and made it the centre of political and intellectual life had she wished, but she cared nothing for politics or ideas. She enjoyed giving a brilliant ball; she enjoyed being the centre-piece of a magnificent spectacle; but an organised social life bored her. She liked to live with her own small circle behind closed doors. Lady Bessborough had pictured the widowed "Mad. Le Clerc" as a heroic young Roman matron who had followed her husband, for love, to danger and death in distant parts. When she met Paulette she was disillusioned. "She is very pretty, had many lovers."

While leading members of London society were enjoying themselves hugely in this startling new Paris they had not seen for so long, the English Ambassador and his wife were having a very difficult time. Lord Whitworth had been named Ambassador in September 1802, six months after the peace treaty, but did not arrive in Paris until November 16th. Now a man of fifty, he had previously been Minister to Poland and for twelve years Ambassador to Russia, had been elevated to the peerage in 1800, and in 1801 had married the widow of the Duke of Dorset. The French had rather hoped for Lord Cornwallis, the chief British negotiator at Amiens, who, as Napoleon's secretary Méneval records, had "fully justified his reputation for fair dealing" and had impressed them when, on the eve of the conclusion of the negotiations, he had refused to put forward demands for last-minute changes as instructed from home. Instead of Lord Cornwallis, Mr. Anthony Merry, Lord Cornwallis's secretary at Amiens, "a man difficult to deal with and full of English reserve", according to Méneval — was sent to Paris to take charge of the Embassy pending Lord Whitworth's arrival. Merry had presented his credentials to Bonaparte on April 18, 1802, and left Paris the following September.

"Lord Whitworth and the Duchess," as, according to the vogue of the day, she called Lady Whitworth, "do everything to offend and show the French every slight in their power," recorded Lady Bessborough. Her opinion was shared by Madame Junot, who conceded that the Ambassador was a fine-looking man with a handsome face but considered him and his wife very haughty. Lady Bessborough added that they were very unpopular with their compatriots as well. When Lord Bessborough finally said that they must go home, the Ambassador's help was enlisted for the charter of a French ship to cross the Channel. But Whitworth was unhelpful, saying that he could not press the matter for fear of a rebuff from the Government. If only they would construct the tunnel under the Channel for which a French engineer had submitted plans to Napoleon! All this seemed unsatisfactory to Lady Bessborough. She liked the new rulers of France, or at least the generals and the politicians, though in the end she became critical of Bonaparte, writing of his despotism and restless ambition and sympathising with Joséphine, the neglected wife. But she cannot have known the difficulties of Whitworth's mission, how demanding they were, and how little time he had for the smart society of Paris or the importunities of his compatriots.

Whitworth, in fact, had an impossible task. It became increasingly clear that for Napoleon the peace was a truce to enable him to rally his forces and, now that the hopes of recovering Louisiana and San Domingo had vanished, to resume expansionist moves towards the east as soon as he could. From time to time there were terrible scenes, in which Napoleon tried to frighten or bully the Ambassador. Whitworth, showing commendable discretion and dignity, stood up to these tirades. But he warned London, and the warning was understood. By the spring of 1803 the situation was becoming tense. The English Government decided that a stand must be taken. The ostensible issue was Malta. Under the Treaty of Amiens the English Government had agreed, with misgivings, to withdraw from the island in favour of some neutral power. The French had undertaken to withdraw their forces from Southern Italy. Napoleon insisted that the question of war or peace hung on the English withdrawing from Malta. When the Ambassador pointed out that the French were not carrying out their side of the bargain, the First Consul flew into a rage. Some days later, at a reception for the Diplomatic Corps, Napoleon upbraided Whitworth: "So you are determined to go to war! If you wish to fight, I will fight also. You may perhaps kill France, but will never intimidate her!" "We wish neither one nor the other," replied the Ambassador. "We wish to live on good terms with her."

The government, anxious to avoid a rupture but deeply concerned by Napoleon's bellicose attitude and what they knew of his designs on the east, were clear that England could not afford to see the Mediterranean become a French sea and must retain some guarantee of the security of her communications with the east. If Napoleon felt so strongly about Malta being in English hands let him—in the words of the Cabinet's instructions to Whitworth—"suggest some other equivalent security". Napoleon did not react to this suggestion, and at the end of April 1803 Whitworth received instructions to inform the French Government that he was to leave Paris if the English terms were not accepted within seven days. Napoleon flew into a rage, Joseph did all he could to avoid a rupture, but nothing came of his efforts. When, on May 2, the seven-day period ran out, with no response from the French side, Whitworth sent for his passports. The French delayed sending them and efforts to reach a settlement continued. On May 11 the French finally rejected the English terms, and the next day the Ambassador left Paris and returned to England. The following week, on May 18, the House of Commons was informed and England and France were once again at war. Paris again became forbidden ground to Lady Bessborough and her friends and was to remain so for more than a decade. Mr. Joseph Talbot, Secretary of Embassy, remained in Paris, but without official character, until May 24, 1803. After his departure diplomatic relations ceased to exist between England and France until 1814.

The English were correct in concluding that Napoleon was bent on expansion. Leader of a new France, prosperous, with ample resources, self-confident and sure of her destiny as a great nation, he was determined on action. The way to the East was blocked, expansion in the Americas was hardly feasible now that San Domingo had been lost and Louisiana sold to the United States. There remained the invasion of England, the power which stood in Napoleon's path across the world. He turned with energy to the preparation on a vast and thorough scale of this formidable amphibious operation.

And while the batteries were being installed in the Channel

ports, the ports themselves dredged and strengthened, the landing-craft and escort-vessels built, the assault troops trained, and Napoleon careered up and down the road (familiar to modern tourists as Route Nationale 1) to inspect the work and encourage the commanders and men, life went on in Paris without much regard being paid to these warlike preparations, of which most of the Parisians were unaware.

8. Second Marriage
1803

WITH THE APPROACH OF SUMMER THE SOCIAL ROUND IN Paris was slowing down and Paulette was becoming bored and restless. Joseph and Signora Letizia, knowing their Paulette, were convinced that she must be found a new husband, or there would be trouble. Napoleon needed little persuasion and gave the matter careful thought. Marriages in his family were now affairs of state. In 1802 while Paulette was in San Domingo, Louis had been unwillingly but suitably married to Joséphine's daughter, Hortense de Beauharnais. Lucien, as always, went his own way. Napoleon was furious when for the second time he contracted a thoroughly unsuitable marriage, this time (three years after the death of his first wife Catherine Boyer) to a young widow of twenty-five whose background and reputation were equally dubious. Her father, Monsieur de Bleschamps, *Commissaire de la Marine*, had died ruined. Her husband, an *agent de change* named Jouberthon, as a result of money difficulties had fled to San Domingo, where he had perished of yellow fever. Alexandrine Jouberthon herself had the reputation of a *femme galante*. Napoleon was outraged. Coming at a moment (in 1803) when he was reaching for supreme power and looked to his brothers and sisters to contract dynastic alliances in accordance with his personal choice and policy requirements, this marriage was the last straw. In April 1804 he ordered Lucien and his bride to leave France.

The nineteen-year-old Jérôme, the youngest member of the family, had also disgraced himself by marrying an American girl, Elizabeth Patterson, whom he met in the United States in 1803 when serving in the French navy. But Jérôme was made of more malleable stuff and the following year, in compliance with his brother's instructions, he annulled the marriage and three years later married a European princess, Catherine of Württemberg, an eminently suitable alliance, on the strength of which he became King of Westphalia.

Paulette in her way was just as headstrong and wilful as Lucien. She must not be allowed to make some frivolous match unworthy of the honour of the Family. Her new husband must be a man of weight and importance whose marriage to a Bonaparte would carry political advantages. With these considerations in mind Napoleon offered his sister's hand to an Italian, who, influential as he must have seemed to Napoleon at the time, is unknown to history apart from this brief connection with the Bonapartes. Count Francesco Melzi d'Eril resided at Milan and was Vice-President of the recently created Italian Republic of which Napoleon himself was President. A fifty-year-old bachelor, he had seen enough of Paulette at Milan in the late seventeen-nineties to be sure that the honour of becoming the First Consul's brother-in-law was too high a price to pay for the disruption of his calm celibate life. Melzi d'Eril excused himself.

Before Napoleon could think of another candidate chance produced the ideal suitor, or so it seemed when he appeared one spring day on Paulette's horizon at Mortefontaine. This was Prince Camillo Borghese.

The Prince, at this time twenty-eight years old, since the death of his father in 1800 had been head of one of the greatest of Italian families, possessor of vast properties in Italy, a splendid palace in Rome, a famous collection of statues and pictures and a princely income. Known as a francophil since the days of Napoleon's first Italian campaign, he felt ill at ease in Italy and, fired by enthusiasm for the republican experiment in France, had come to Paris in the spring of 1803, thinking to live in France. Tall, slim and exquisitely dressed, he took Paris by storm, with his name, his manners, the general splendour of his way of living. His carriages and horses were more elegant than anything that had been seen since the Bourbons. He was the first man, as Madame Junot noted with her eye for style, to appear at a Parisian reception in full evening dress (*"en habit habillé"*). The portrait by the fashionable painter Gérard depicts him as a strikingly handsome young man, tall, with thick wavy black hair and black side-whiskers, clean-shaven, with a sensitive mouth slightly open to reveal fine white teeth; dressed in a splendid coat covered with gold embroidery, a velvet and silk-lined cloak, also heavily embroidered in gold, thrown over his left shoulder, a high collar with lace ruff and stock, and a fine pair of legs in knee breeches and white stockings. Altogether a young magnifico with all the qualifications—lineage, wealth, good looks, loyalty to France—to make him a worthy consort for the sister of Napoleon. So thought Napoleon when the Papal legate presented Borghese. Paulette herself was automatically attracted to the brilliant young stranger from Rome who had made such a sensation in the Paris salons. What none of them had discovered was that, for all his position and appearance, Camillo Borghese rarely had a thought in his head beyond the management of a team of horses and the expensive pleasures of a rich Roman aristocrat.

In his casual way Camillo had allowed his life in Paris to be managed by a certain Cavaliere Angiolini, finding it useful to rely on a compatriot who knew the Parisian scene to advise him in connection with his entry into French society. Angiolini had been the representative in Paris from 1795 to 1798 of the Grand Duchy of Tuscany until the disappearance of this principality as a result of the creation of the Cisalpine Republics after Napoleon's defeat of the Austrians, and had stayed on in Paris in a shadowy capacity looking after the deposed Grand Duke's interests. It was Angiolini who introduced Camillo to Joseph, whom he had known in Rome in earlier days. Joseph and Napoleon talked matters over and decided that Camillo would be a suitable husband for Paulette, and Joseph asked Angiolini to sound out the Prince.

Camillo's first reaction was completely negative. He was not in the least in love with Paulette and had no desire to make a great political marriage. Angiolini, dismayed but determined to bring off a stroke so much to his advantage, enlisted the help of the Papal legate, who saw advantage for the Holy See in an alliance between a sister of Napoleon and a great Roman prince. Eventually, on Midsummer Day 1803, Angiolini was able to write in triumph to Joseph: *"L'affaire est faite.* Prince Borghese will be only too happy if the First Consul will grant him the honour of taking as wife your very charming sister, Madame Paulette." He added that Camillo asked only for one favour; the time to apprise his mother, the old Princess Borghese, before the news became public knowledge. The ease with which Camillo had been persuaded to do the precise opposite of what he wanted to do—it had taken Angiolini and the Papal legate only three weeks to effect this transformation!—is a clue to the weakness of character of the man who was to be Paulette's husband, for better for worse, during the next twenty-two years. Everybody was delighted by the news—Paulette, Napoleon, the Family and the Pope. In Royalist circles it was said that at last there was a real princess in the Bonaparte family.

Under the new Civil Code Madame Leclerc was legally obliged to observe ten months of widowhood before remarrying. Hitherto one year and six weeks had been accepted as the conventional period. Leclerc had died during the night of November 1-2, 1802. The earliest legal date on which the marriage could take place was therefore early September, and in accordance with tradition mid-December would have been thought generally more suitable. But Paulette was impatient. She had never paid much attention to rules and regulations. Napoleon intervened and decreed that, despite the new ten-month rule, the ceremony should not take place before the expiry of a full year. As a concession, he agreed to waive the six weeks. In the meanwhile, the business arrangements for the future marriage were settled and formulated in an agreement which Paulette and Camillo both signed before a notary on August 23.

On August 28 Paulette and Camillo were married at Mortefontaine in great secrecy by an Italian priest in the presence of Joseph, Lucien and Angiolini. The secret was well kept. Even Napoleon, who assumed that his instructions would be obeyed and that the marriage would not take place till November, heard nothing about the secret ceremony for several weeks. When the facts came out, as they were bound to do as time went on and it became clear that nothing was being arranged for the expected ceremony, he was justifiably incensed. But the match was so advantageous and Paulette so unpredictable that for once he swallowed his wrath and nothing more was said.

It remains a mystery why Paulette acted with such precipitation. She had only to wait five more days to be within the legal ten-month period, and with the law on her side she could have defied Napoleon to prove why she should wait when only old-fashioned tradition required this longer period. Paulette may have done it simply to show she could defy her brother and the world at large. Signora Letizia at one point encouraged Paulette not to delay. Or it may have been a sudden caprice, since it seems from a message Camillo sent in haste to Angiolini that the decision was taken on the spur of the moment. Perhaps it was the same spontaneous sensual urge as that which was to impel Napoleon to consummate his union with Marie Louise at Compiègne after the marriage by proxy and before the state marriage ceremony. The blood of the Bonapartes ran strong. Whatever the reasoning, or lack of it, the gesture was typical of the capricious and wilful Paulette.

9. Camillo Borghese
1803-4

"MADAME LA PRINCESSE DE BORGHESE"—THIS FORMAL
opening disturbed Paulette as she went on to decipher her
brother's execrable handwriting. The letter was written from
Boulogne, where Napoleon was inspecting the invasion preparations, and was dated November 11, 1803, six weeks after
the furtive marriage ceremony. She knew only too well how
much she had annoyed him, first by ignoring his wishes about
the date of her marriage, and later by refusing to go and take up
residence in Rome. It had never occurred to Paulette that Rome
was the proper place for the wife of a Roman prince to live, or
at least to visit. Her plan was quite different. She intended to
live in Paris, to make herself the centre of all that was gayest
and most brilliant in this new exciting society, and to make her
own court at the Hôtel de Charost far more attractive and
splendid than Joséphine's at the Tuileries. Her anxiety cannot
have decreased as she slowly made out the following.

"The bad season is upon us," she read, "the Alps will be
covered in snow, so leave for Rome. Make a point of being
charming and considerate to the ladies, relations and friends of
your husband's family. More is expected of you than anyone
else. Above all, conform to the customs of the country, never
criticise anything, admire everything, and do not say: 'In Paris
we have better than that.' Show much attachment and respect
towards the Holy Father whom I like very much and who,
from the simplicity of his habits, is worthy of the post he occupies.
What I shall most enjoy hearing from reports that reach me about
you is that your behaviour is good. The only nation you must
never receive are the English, so long as we are at war, and you

must never admit them to your company. Love your husband, make a happy household, and above all do not be wanton and capricious. You are twenty-four, you ought by now to be mature and sensible. [Actually, she was just twenty-three in November 1803.] I am fond of you and will always take pleasure in learning that you are happy."

Paulette can hardly have appreciated these home truths from a brother who knew her weaknesses only too well; but even she understood that in face of such a formal instruction, there was nothing to do but submit. Three days later, in their travelling berline and accompanied by a large train of attendants, she and Camillo left on the long journey to Rome. If she must undertake this unwelcome removal, at least she was determined to take it in slow stages and get as much enjoyment as possible from the important position she now occupied.

Once across the border it was a triumphal progress. At Florence, now the capital of the kingdom of Etruria, they stayed in one of Camillo's many Italian residences and were received with great ceremony by the widowed queen. At Arezzo, Chiusi, Orte, there were receptions, balls, banquets, and all along the line of their route crowds of enthusiastic townsfolk and villagers—a princely progress. After they crossed the frontier of the Papal States, they were escorted from stage to stage by guards of honour. At last, at nine o'clock on a dark December evening, the berline drew up before the torchlit façade of the Palazzo Salviati (where Camillo lived during the widowhood of his mother). Paulette's first visit, naturally, was to the Dowager Princess and the Borghese family at the Palazzo Borghese. They received Camillo's French bride with open arms.

Napoleon's injunctions had gone home, and Paulette's début in Rome could not have been more dutiful and correct. After a few days' delay because her new dresses had not arrived from Paris, she went to see the Pope. The meeting was a success on both sides. For all her frivolity there was a deep-seated vein of religious feeling in Paulette's complex character. From now on the friendship of this Pope, Pius VII, and later, during the last two years of her life, that of Pope Leo XII, was to stand her in good stead.

There were two magnificent receptions on successive days at the Palazzo Borghese. Paulette charmed all she met—cardinals, ambassadors, Roman aristocrats. The Cardinal Secretary of State wrote to the Nuncio in Paris: "This lady is really very gracious, very agreeable, with the most charming manners." Napoleon, pleased by what he heard from the Nuncio and Fesch, wrote personally to the Pope asking him to be kind to "Madame Paulette" and to give her the benefit of his counsel.

As the excitement of her first arrival wore off Paulette began to be restless and homesick. She found the great Roman palaces oppressive and depressing. The Roman aristocracy seemed to think she was only interested in statuary. She knew nothing of Roman history or classical art, or Renaissance art for that matter. In any case it was all very different from France. She longed for the malice and gaiety, the heady excitement of Paris. She wanted to turn her back on the chiaroscuro of Roman interiors with their profusion of marble statues and pilasters, and return to the mirrors and silks of the charming salons in her beloved Faubourg St. Honoré. She heard with envy and frustration of the brilliant life of her relatives in Paris.

Then there was Camillo. She had adored Camillo at first sight, with his good looks, his manners of the *grand seigneur*, his beautiful clothes. She had been impressed to find what a great position he and his family held in Italy. Everything seemed per-fect, till it was gradually borne in on her that Camillo was a bore and a dullard, a man of no depth of mind or character. It was painful to spend an evening alone in his company. His mind rarely rose above talk about horses, hunting, or the affairs of his vast estates. All this might have been supportable if Camillo had been able to give Paulette what she really needed more than anything else. It was some months before she brought herself to face the unbelievable truth. "I would rather," she burst out to Laure Junot, "have remained the widow of General Leclerc, with an income of 20,000 francs, than have become the wife of

77

a eunuch!" The term may have been an exasperated exagger-
ation, but Camillo's lack of ardour was well-known to his contemporaries, one of whom (General Thiébault) confirmed that
he was no more adequate as a husband than he had been as a
lover. Camillo evidently fell short of expectations, for the Bonapartes, a passionate race, looked for equal qualities in their
consorts. Joséphine's hold over Napoleon lasted because she
knew how to make herself physically attractive to him. It was
a dreadful moment for Paulette when she realised that Camillo
could never make her happy. Had he been able to do so and
satisfy her instinct for maternity, her life would have been
happier, perhaps longer, and certainly less aimless.

For a spirited young woman of twenty-three this was a fatal
bar to the success of a union which in other respects provided
all she could desire—great wealth, great position, a magnifico
for a husband. Rumours that all was not going well in the
young ménage filtered through to Paris. Paulette herself, as
early as the end of February, was writing disconsolately to her
brother-in-law Murat: "I should so much like to leave Italy
for a little so as to see my family and my beloved France. I always
have a cold here . . . Please do not forget your sister Bonaparte-
Borghese." Poor Paulette—disillusioned with her glittering
husband, bored with Roman society, desperately homesick for
Paris, shivering and ill in mid-winter in the Roman palaces
which were now to be her home.

When this unsatisfactory state of affairs was reported to
Napoleon, he launched one of his famous thunderbolts. Complaining that he had felt obliged to take time off from "great
affairs" in order to write to her, he told her (April 6, 1804) to
"love your husband and your family, be prudent, accommodate
yourself to the customs of the City of Rome, and get it well
fixed in your head that if, at your age, you give way to bad
counsels, you can no longer count on me. As to Paris, you can
be sure that there you will find no support and that I will never
receive you there except with your husband. If you break
with him, the fault will be yours, and then France will be

forbidden to you. You will forfeit your happiness and my friendship."

Napoleon was not the only one to intervene with the object of holding together a marriage whose break-up would be a serious political embarrassment. Angiolini, the go-between, who had received a long, childish letter of complaint from Camillo, told him that he must learn to manage Paulette and, above all, give her a son. Angiolini had perfectly understood what was needed to make Paulette happy.

When Napoleon grumbled to Paulette that she had made him switch his mind from great affairs, he was alluding to the plan which he had been weighing for some time to assume the throne as Emperor of the French. After the consolidation of his gains from Austria under the peace of Lunéville in 1801, followed by the uneasy truce with England, the renunciation of his transatlantic ambitions after the loss of San Domingo and the signing of the Louisiana Purchase, Napoleon had contented himself with the maintenance of a legal state of war with England and with ostentatiously warlike preparations for invasion. In the interval he had completed the reorganisation of France under a centralised system. This took shape in the form of three great Codes, legal, commercial and civil, of which the Civil Code—the Code Napoléon—was of by far the greatest significance for the destinies of France. Its underlying conception was the retention of the ancient customs of France, passed through the alchemy of the Revolution and remoulded into a modern shape, paternalistic, authoritarian and inflexible. What the French people wanted, Napoleon believed, was not liberty but equality. He therefore gave them a system under which there was equality of opportunity, and talent was harnessed to the needs of the State. But individual initiative was systematically repressed. The whole great machine of State was controlled by Napoleon, to whom every citizen was expected to look as the leader. Looking back from exile on his achievements, Napoleon claimed that his government was a kind of republic. He had always held that sovereignty lay in the people. His maxim was *la carrière est ouverte à tous les talents.*

There was deep anxiety in England about the course of events in France. The English Government could hardly view with equanimity a neighbour across the Channel under the personal leadership of a man whose world-wide ambitions were undisguised and who was openly preparing the invasion of the British Isles. In France, too, there were violent opponents of Napoleon's authoritarian aims. Some were genuine democrats who hated him for his betrayal of the principles of the Revolution; others were staunch loyalists devoted to the Bourbon cause; others again were rogues in English pay. Since Napoleon had become First Consul plots and conspiracies followed thick and fast. The crisis came early in 1804, by when it was apparent to many that his aim was the throne. In a last desperate throw, a band of Royalist conspirators, of whom the ringleaders were Cadoudal and the former Republican general Pichegru, came to Paris with the object of overthrowing Napoleon. The English Government seems to have been implicated. The ringleaders were captured, but the event, coming just at the moment when he had decided to ascend the throne, caused Napoleon to lose his habitual balance. He was convinced, or allowed others to convince him, that the success of the conspiracy would have been followed by the entry into France of a young Bourbon prince, the Duc d'Enghien, and the assumption by the Prince of the government. The Duke, to his misfortune, was at that moment staying in Baden, near the French frontier. French agents crossed the border, kidnapped him in bed and rushed him to Paris. After being held for two hours at the Porte de la Villette, he was taken to the fortress of Vincennes. There he was summarily tried in secret and shot the same night.

There is no doubt that Napoleon personally organised the kidnapping and ordered the summary trial. Whether he ordered the Duke's execution is open to doubt. What is certain is that, in the circumstances, the Duke must have seemed like the centre-piece of a conspiracy, and his defiance must have confirmed his

The Comte de Forbin. Drawing by Ingres   Pauline Bonaparte. Sketch by David
Photo Bulloz   *Collection Germain Seligman*

The British Embassy in Paris, the former Hôtel de Charost, seen
from the garden and showing the two wings added by Pauline
Photo Bulloz

Pauline Bonaparte by Lefèvre, ca. 1809

Cliché des Musées Nationaux

guilt in the eyes of the tribunal. Méneval has described the tense scenes in the Tuileries when the plans for the kidnapping were perfected, and the distress of Napoleon, whether simulated or real, when he heard of the execution. In a large room used as a bedroom by Louis XVI and by Napoleon when Emperor, the First Consul, the Minister of War and Méneval were bending over a map, illuminated by the light of two three-branched candelabra. Napoleon, compass in hand, marked out the kidnap route and dictated instructions which Méneval wrote down. After the report of the execution was brought to him in the library at Malmaison, Napoleon abruptly said, "It is well." After a moment, he left the room and Méneval heard him walking slowly up the staircase that led to the little room over the library. He shut himself up there and did not reappear for a long time. Talleyrand remarked that the execution of the Duc d'Enghien was worse than a crime, it was a blunder. Napoleon himself, at St. Helena eleven years later, considered that "the Duc d'Enghien's well-merited death injured Napoleon in public opinion and was of no political use whatever to him".

Two months later, on May 18, 1804, Napoleon was proclaimed Emperor of the French. On the 20th it was announced that the Emperor's brothers and sisters would receive the title of Imperial Highness. Paulette's first act was for the second time to change her name slightly but significantly. Paoletta-Paulette was now Her Imperial Highness Princess Pauline Borghese.

But the enjoyment of her new and exalted position quickly wore off and she longed all the more to leave Rome for Paris. Yet even she did not dare to flout Napoleon's direct instruction. Now that he was Emperor she was in fact less inclined to do so. From this time onwards, according to her own lights, she was a faithful subject. The Emperor's word was law—in theory at all events.

Her relations with Camillo became more and more strained. The family, on both sides, took a hand. The Dowager Princess Borghese naturally supported her son. Signora Letizia and Lucien, who arrived together in Rome in June, took Pauline's part. The Signora, for all her personal austerity, her puritanical standards, her disapproval of the extravagant luxury with which her family were now surrounding themselves, had been indulgent to a point of irresponsibility towards this daughter. In the difficult early days she had never made any determined effort to discipline the little Paoletta. She was even less inclined to exercise any maternal influence over the young woman who was now Princess Pauline Borghese. She had no high opinion of Camillo, and at this particular time was irritated with Napoleon. He had thought to please his mother by decreeing that she should have not only the style of Imperial Highness (that was perfectly suitable), but also the special title of "Madame Mère". Letizia, who was to go down in history under this name, did not see herself in the rôle of a sanctified matriarch. She disliked the French language. She did not like the French. She far preferred being called "La Signora". As for Camillo, he resigned himself to keeping up the outward appearance of the marriage and consoled himself by writing long complaining letters to Angiolini. The union which had started so ecstatically was already set in the mould of indifference in which it was to remain for twenty years until the halcyon sunset of its last few months.

By summer Pauline fell seriously ill, from frustration or the onset of the weakening of her constitution which plagued and brought her to a premature death. Accompanied by her doctor, Peyre, who had remained tenaciously by her side since San Domingo days when he had been chief medical officer to the expeditionary force, she and Camillo set out for Pisa to drink the waters. The cure did her no good, and it was decided to try the baths at Lucca. There she was joined by the Signora. They lived a retired life at this fashionable watering-place, disappointing the local society and the shopkeepers who had been expecting the Imperial ladies to receive in suitable style, spend a lot of money and thus add to the revenues of the citizens. Pauline must have been thoroughly out-of-sorts to live, for the first time in her active young life, in semi-retirement. To crown all, her little boy was suddenly taken ill with convulsions and died. Dermid had been left behind at Mondragone near Frascati, and

the news was concealed from Pauline for several days because
of the low state of her health. When it was gently broken to
her, her grief was shattering. It was the severing of the last tie
with a comparatively happy past and accentuated the bleakness
of the future. In the depth of her grief and despair she once
again, following the old Corsican custom, cut off her hair and
cast it on the little coffin as she had done in San Domingo on his
father's death.

This was a desperate period for Pauline, disillusioned with
her husband, bereaved of the one little human being for whom
she felt deep affection, bullied by her overbearing brother. She
could not go to Paris and would not go to Rome. It was with
unbelievable relief that she received permission in October to
return to Paris. This was no act of compassion on the part of
Napoleon. He needed his sister in Paris, with her husband and
other members of the family, for the grandiose ceremony of his
coronation as Emperor of the French.

10. Her Imperial Highness
1804

THE PARIS TO WHICH PAULINE RETURNED IN THE AUTUMN of 1804 had suffered a sea-change during the twelve months of her absence. It was even more exuberant, brilliant and full of movement, charmed to find itself overnight an Imperial city. All looked to the dynamic man of thirty-five who presided over the destinies of the French. A strict protocol now regimented the life of the court and society. On becoming Emperor, Napoleon had sent for his secretary and requested to be shown the precedents under the Monarchy. The purely decorative and time-consuming practices of the past were rejected. There was no court of professional courtiers intriguing for the sovereign's favour, and when some of the members of Louis XVI's former personal bodyguard offered themselves as a Garde du Corps, Napoleon refused their services. Nevertheless, courts were held and everyone was expected to behave and to be suitably dressed. The Emperor had to be approached with decorum and restraint, whether in person or in writing. But the absurdities of the *ancien régime* were jettisoned. It was no longer necessary for the writer of a submission to the sovereign to measure the height at which the first line of the document might be begun, the number of times "Your Majesty" might be used, or other minute details which were formerly matters of rigorous etiquette.

As an Imperial Highness, Pauline found that she had been allotted apartments in the Château of St. Cloud and went with pleasure to live in this palace, with its magnificent park on the hills above the Seine, within easy driving distance of the centre of Paris, while she was embellishing her own house in the rue du Faubourg St. Honoré and assembling the members of her household. As one of the Emperor's sisters she had to have a house-hold—secretaries, ladies-in-waiting, a chaplain. This was exciting and grand; but soon the novelty wore off. She complained that the air of St. Cloud was too strong, and her apartments uncomfortable. So off she and the patient Camillo went to the Petit Trianon, the charming small villa built by Louis XV at Versailles which Napoleon lent her.

Napoleon himself generally resided in the Tuileries, in the centre of Paris, and later on at the Elysée. He also paid regular visits to St. Cloud, Compiègne, Rambouillet, where he gave great hunting parties, and Fontainebleau, where the stay of the court lasted for six or eight weeks in September and October. Wherever he went, the work of government went with him. Having completed his reorganisation of the French state and solemnised his own position by the coronation of December 2, 1804, he was working to bring his plans for the invasion of England to a head. Sometimes, according to his *Secrétaire du Portefeuille*, Méneval, he would brood for days on end without doing any regular work. These periods of cogitation would be followed by bursts of intense activity, sometimes in the middle of the night, when Napoleon would come into his study "in his white dressing-gown with a Madras handkerchief round his head", call for Méneval and dictate instructions, refreshing himself from time to time with sherbet and ices. Practically every detail of home, foreign and military affairs passed through his hands. He preferred to initiate action himself, and paid little attention to recommendations from his ministers and staff. "Napoleon," records Méneval, "used to call not answering the best part of his work." He preferred to dictate to his secretaries and rarely wrote himself—"only when he happened to be alone and had to put the first rush of an idea on paper. His writing was unreadable, he could not read his own writing again. His orthography left much to be desired."

Besides Méneval, Napoleon employed two other secretaries, Bourrienne and Fain. Louis-Antoine Fauvelet de Bourrienne had been at school with Napoleon at Brienne and was his exact contemporary. In 1797 Napoleon, who had a sentimental affection for his friends of schoolboy days, invited Bourrienne, then at the beginning of a career in diplomacy, to be his *secrétaire intime* during the first Italian campaign. Bourrienne stayed with Napoleon till 1804. It soon became apparent to Napoleon that his secretary was a scoundrel. He closed his eyes to Bourrienne's underhand dealings on behalf of Joséphine, who was acquiring jewellery without his knowledge, but when he became involved in a financial scandal concerning public money Napoleon felt obliged to dismiss him. Even so, he found him an honourable if not distinguished post as Chargé d'Affaires of the Legation at Hamburg. In that post he lined his purse and intrigued with the Bourbons. Napoleon, perfectly aware that he was being cheated and betrayed, took no action beyond an occasional remonstrance, and left Bourrienne undisturbed at Hamburg till the end. At the Restoration Bourrienne offered his services to Louis XVIII and was made a Minister of State. His memoirs, published in 1829-31, are full of disloyalties to his former chief and benefactor.

The job of Agathon Jean-François Fain was that of official historian and archivist, his title *Secrétaire Archiviste Particulier de l'Empereur*. Appointed in 1806 at the age of twenty-eight, he accompanied Napoleon on all his campaigns to Waterloo and the end. He later wrote his own interesting version of events, and did not accept service after the Restoration until 1830, when Louis Philippe made him First Secretary of the Cabinet.

Claude-François de Méneval, who like Fain was created a Baron of the Empire and like him was born in 1778, entered Napoleon's service in 1802 and was also with him to the end. Of the three secretaries he was the one who handled current business and saw Napoleon at work at all hours of the day, whether in France or abroad on the campaigns where he usually accompanied the Emperor. "I almost killed poor Méneval," Napoleon was to remark at St. Helena. His memoirs, completed and published by his son in 1849, are precise, descriptive and imbued with a wholly loyal, even uncritical, admiration for the man he served.

The secretaries, a Belgian valet and a negro bodyguard, were the small private staff with whom Napoleon lived and worked. As a supreme master of the use of outward display for political ends, and fully conscious of the need for the Emperor of the French to present a glittering image at home and abroad, he surrounded himself with ceremonial and protocol in his public appearances. But the ceremonial was cut to a minimum. As the sole ruler of France he needed all the time he could have for the endless hours of work of government and reform at home, the boundless schemes of conquest and domination. His personal tastes remained simple, even austere. He dressed simply even on ceremonial occasions (though his coronation was an exception). The Parisian tailors complained that he spent too little on clothes. He ate little, drank nothing but a little red wine (Chambertin) diluted with water. He liked to have few people around him. The horde of courtiers, the Byzantine intricacies of the Bourbon court were abolished. Most of his waking hours were spent with Méneval, Fain and (until his disgrace) Bourrienne, with Constant his valet in attendance during the day, and the negro Rustam who slept outside his bedroom door at night. To this small circle of intimate attendants he was the kindest and most considerate of masters, though after his fall Bourrienne betrayed his memory, Constant by his own account failed to follow the fallen Emperor into exile because of the lack of opportunity to do so, and Rustam, whom Napoleon had received as a present from the Sheikh of Cairo during the Egyptian expedition, lost faith in his master after the first abdication, refused to go with him to Elba, was imprisoned during the Hundred Days and ended his life in misery in England.

Méneval was fascinated by Napoleon's methods of work, which he recorded in great detail. While he had no set hours during the twenty-four for work, meals or sleep, he recognised the need for a certain minimum of routine and ceremony. As a general rule Méneval used to come in with the documents and news of the day while the Emperor was dressing in the morning. Napoleon would listen and dictate instructions. Corvisart, his principal medical adviser and an excellent doctor, was often present at these early morning sessions in Napoleon's bedroom. Though there was no exceptional weakness or incapacity in Napoleon's physical constitution, his expenditure of nervous energy took an early toll. He knew this, and was concerned about his increasing corpulence despite vigorous exercise and abstemious habits.

Corvisart no doubt shook his head as Napoleon continued to transact business with his secretary even as he shaved himself, Constant holding up a small mirror and turning it as required. In an age where people of importance were shaved by an attendant, Napoleon, as he recalled on his death-bed, was proud of having up till then performed that office for himself. Like all the Bonapartes he was fond of baths (his bathrooms at Fontaine-bleau and other palaces are familiar to modern tourists). If he felt he had no time for a bath he doused himself with water from a large silver basin and was rubbed down by Constant with eau-de-Cologne. Méneval adds the detail that his flannel singlets, his vests and pants, were changed every day. At nine o'clock he held a levée. This was not a ceremonial occasion as it used to be under the *ancien régime*, but a strictly business meeting to enable him to give instructions to Ministers and officials. It was rare that any discussion developed or was allowed.

Napoleon used to snatch a hasty lunch, which rarely lasted more than ten minutes, in a little salon next to his study, and return immediately to work. Once a week, on Wednesdays at noon, he presided over the Council of Ministers. Dinner was at 6 p.m. If busy, Napoleon would give this meal a miss, but usually he dined alone with Joséphine, except on Wednesdays when the Ministers stayed to dinner after the Council and on Sundays when there was a family party. Napoleon ate and drank frugally, and allowed himself one cup of coffee after meals. He usually spent an hour or so with the Empress after dinner and then returned to work. Once a week, after dinner, his librarian came along with the new books. Napoleon would sit at his desk, glance over them, "throwing on the ground or pitching into the fire those which did not interest him, or which displeased him, and putting one or two—rarely three—aside to read with greater attention". He was a voracious reader, and took a travelling library with him on campaigns. In his youth Rousseau was his hero. When he became a ruler, intellectuals were the curse of the earth.

When not abroad Napoleon used to shoot or hunt almost every week, "less from inclination," says Méneval, "than for the sake of exercise". He had a wide choice of splendid royal hunting forests—some close to Paris—St. Cloud, St. Germain, Versailles; others further afield—Rambouillet, Fontainebleau and Compiègne.

What were Pauline's feelings towards her brother when she joined a Sunday evening family party at St. Cloud or one of the other Imperial country residences? Did she find, in this masterful, imperious potentate of thirty-five, any trace of the intense young lieutenant of seventeen whom she had idolised at first sight at the age of six in Ajaccio? The appearance was not very different. The Emperor of the French wore a uniform almost as plain as that of a cadet, white vest and pantaloons, white silk stockings, with the green coat of the *chasseurs de la garde* on weekdays, and for the Sunday parties a blue coat with white lapels. He was not so slim as in his cadet days and was already acquiring the familiar stocky, paunchy figure of his innumerable portraits. But the real transformation was in his features, now stamped with power and decision. As many of his contemporaries noted, his eyes, when he was aroused, flashed glances that struck terror in those at whom they were aimed. His smile, when he was in an agreeable mood, was very attractive.

Often as she infuriated him by her inconsequence, he had a warm feeling for Pauline, and Pauline, for her part, admired and respected him for what he was, or rather for the supreme position he held, even when she considered his interference with her private life unwarrantable. For Pauline politics were of no interest, but the will of the Emperor was something she accepted. Stories were current in France and in England that Napoleon was so fond of her, and she so complaisant to her brother, that their relations were actually incestuous. The two principal sources of these stories were Joséphine and Fouché, the one almost insane with hatred of Pauline and jealousy of Napoleon as she saw the day of divorce approaching, the other towards the end Napoleon's most bitter political opponent. Industrious retailers of court gossip like Madame de Rémusat, Joséphine's lady-in-waiting and close friend, uncritically reproduced the rumour, which was eagerly spread by royalist propaganda anxious to denigrate the Bonaparte family. Joséphine certainly so far lost control on one occasion as to make a direct accusation to Napoleon's face, which nearly precipitated the divorce. Nothing in the characters of Napoleon or Pauline suggests any trace of perversion. Both were by nature amorous, but in a normal way. When it was a question of helping Napoleon in a love-affair, however, Pauline could be complaisant enough. After his divorce from Joséphine and before his marriage to Marie Louise of Austria, his roving eye fell on Madame de Mathis, one of Pauline's ladies-in-waiting, who was showing reluctance. "Do you not know," said Pauline, "that one must never say No to the Emperor?" The story is told by Laure Junot, who added that Pauline went on to say: "Were he to tell me that he desired me, I would forget I was his sister and reply: 'Your Majesty, I am yours to command.'" If Pauline ever made such a remark, it was certainly made in mock solemnity. This indiscretion was, of course, repeated and has been handed down in the biographies, much to the discredit of Pauline. The evidence for an unnatural relationship between Pauline and Napoleon has been examined by several eminent writers, notably Lévy, Turquand, Kühn and Masson. All dismiss the stories as calumnies.

The Family, as has been seen, had taken a dislike to Joséphine from the outset, and Joséphine had not helped to secure her position by her chronic infidelities. After eight years of marriage to Napoleon she had failed to produce an heir, a fact which the Bonapartes exploited to the utmost at the time of the Coronation

when the need to perpetuate the dynasty became of first importance. Pauline was the most active in pressing Napoleon to
divorce the faithless Créole. She had never forgiven Joséphine
for her part in preventing her own marriage to Fréron. The
memory of attempts to humiliate her rankled. She still quivered
with annoyance when she recalled Joséphine's behaviour the day
she had, unwillingly enough, paid a formal call after her marriage
to Borghese on the wife of the First Consul at St. Cloud. She
had presented herself in a grand dress of green velvet, wearing
the magnificent Borghese diamonds. Joséphine had managed to
find out to the last detail how her sister-in-law would be dressed,
and, wearing a very simple muslin gown, received her in a salon
which she had specially arranged with furniture and hangings in
blue. Still, at that time, Pauline was a princess, the only one in
the family, and Joséphine was merely Madame Bonaparte. Now
Joséphine was Empress. It had been only a passing satisfaction
to have pulled so hard on Joséphine's white satin bee-embroidered
train in Notre Dame that she was nearly jerked backwards at the
moment the crown was being placed on her head.

Pauline simply could not understand her brother's reluctance,
on assuming the throne, to rid himself of so unsuitable a consort.
But Napoleon was under the woman's spell. He made tremendous scenes about her infidelities and her fantastic monetary
extravagance. But in the end he always forgave her and paid
the bills. Joséphine, his senior by six years, retained her appeal
for Napoleon even after policy won the day and he had divorced
her in order to marry the Austrian Emperor's daughter. "Poor
Joséphine!" he wrote at Malmaison in 1815 (she had died the
previous year). "I cannot get used to being here without her.
It seems as though I may see her coming out of an alley any
moment, picking some of those flowers that she loved so much!"
Those flowers were roses, of which Joséphine had planted 250
varieties at Malmaison.

Joséphine, though well aware of her hold over Napoleon,
was in a frenzy of anxiety about her position when her husband
became Emperor. Much of her hatred of those trying to dis-

lodge her was directed against Pauline, the spoilt favourite sister. Instinctively, and egged on by Madame de Rémusat, she hit back by retailing to all and sundry stories, real or invented, about Pauline's private life, and she did not hesitate to hit back at Napoleon too by suggesting that he had unmentionable reasons for being indulgent to his sister. The story of Joséphine and Pauline is the story of two women who disliked each other on sight and stooped to any depth of meanness to harm each other.

It was while she was staying at the Petit Trianon that Pauline summoned the artist Antonio Canova, whom she had known in Rome, to come to Paris to make a life-size portrait of her in marble. Canova, a son of working-class parents, had started life as a stonemason and rapidly developed his own individualistic style, a blend of the classical and the romantic with an indefinable quality of voluptuousness. He was in great demand as a court portraitist all over Europe. Napoleon gave him two commissions. One resulted in the well-known bust at Fontainebleau. The other was a colossal statue of the Emperor in the nude holding a diminutive figure of Victory. It was much disliked by Napoleon, and is now in Apsley House, the Duke of Wellington's home in London.

A display of nudity of a classical kind aroused no inhibitions in Pauline. The prevailing fashion was in that direction, though she was perhaps a little ahead of it. The idea of a lightly draped life-size portrait of herself in marble reclining, in the classical manner, on a couch, appealed to her. Who could execute such a portrait better than Canova, past-master in the art of enhancing the contours of a beautiful woman and evoking the dignity befitting a princess? Canova himself, a worldly middle-aged man as well as an uninhibited artist, had doubts about the project. He confessed after the statue had been finished that he had several times suggested to the Princess that she should be represented not as Venus but as Diana. However, the idea of being immortalised in the full dress of a classical huntress was not at all to Pauline's taste. Her features and complexion had suffered from the climate of the West Indies. Her body, slight

and exquisitely moulded, was to retain the contours of youth
for ten or twelve years to come. She wished to be Venus wearing
the minimum of classical drapery.

The idea of such a portrait of Her Imperial Highness was
startling not only to Canova (though once he had reluctantly
agreed to the project he put all his artistic genius into producing
a masterpiece): it shocked everybody. Somebody went so far
as to ask Pauline tentatively whether it was not uncomfortable
to pose so lightly clad. She replied easily that there had been a
fire in the room. Nobody was more shocked and distressed than
Prince Borghese. He had the statue removed to Turin and
later to his palace in Rome (where it still is) and rarely allowed
it to be seen. Much later—in 1818—when she knew that her
tortured body was at last losing its beauty, Pauline wrote to
Camillo begging him to show it to nobody. Like the girl in
Plato's epigram, she no longer desired to look in her mirror
since she did not wish to see herself as she was and could not see
herself as she used to be.

As one of the Emperor's sisters, Pauline had her own court.
The principal personage was a *dame d'honneur*, under whom there
were a number of *dames pour accompagner*. There were three
lectrices dames d'annonce. Besides these ladies, all of good but not
eminent families, there were a number of men in the household,
the chief being a secretary, an *intendant* and a chaplain. Women
and men alike, all had been selected by Napoleon or his advisers.
She also acquired a negro, Paul—no doubt the counterpart in
her mind of Napoleon's Rustam—who acted as her bodyguard
and who had the freedom of the private apartments. The constitution of Her Imperial Highness's court had been announced
in the summer of 1805. Pauline had had no say in the selection
of her courtiers. She found her *dame d'honneur* a bore, but liked
most of the younger ladies. The male members of the court did
their best to do their job but received little co-operation from
the Princess. They complained of her indolence in everything
except matters of dress. As an Imperial Highness she was expected
to be in the height of fashion. Court etiquette required her to

wear the low-cut evening dresses bound high below the breasts which became her so well. The fashionable court colours, white, green or rose, flattered her complexion, and she found that a *parure* of diamonds and pearls, with cameo brooches on her shoulders, suited her to perfection. Leroy's prices were certainly high, but he was a marvellous dressmaker. He charged exorbitantly for Indian muslin and cashmere shawls because the importation of these manufactures of the British Empire was forbidden and they were introduced as contraband. But to be in the fashion Pauline did not hesitate to defy her brother's edicts and to pay Leroy's prices. Even so, she was never crazy about clothes like Joséphine, who ran up enormous bills with Leroy which Napoleon, after a scene, always paid. She merely went along with the vogue in a haphazard way.

The truth was that Pauline was incapable of adopting the kind of orderly and ceremonial routine which this official entourage, following the Emperor's instructions, tried to introduce into her household. She particularly rebelled against the attempts of Duroc, the grand marshal of Napoleon's household, to enforce the instruction that she must submit to him for approval the names of the persons she wished to entertain. Pauline was not made for the carefully thought-out system of the Napoleonic protocol, every feature of which was designed to serve a useful political end.

Pauline, a true Bonaparte, had a strong sense of the value of money and the importance of getting value for money. At this period she was not a particularly rich woman. She had Leclerc's fortune, more than she expected but not large for an Imperial Highness; Napoleon had given her a handsome sum on Leclerc's death, she had what Borghese saw fit to allow her. It was not till Napoleon created her Duchess of Guastalla the following year (1806) that she enjoyed a larger and more regular source of income.

However, with her income of half a million francs Pauline could exercise her considerable taste and administrative ability in making the Hôtel de Charost a suitable residence for a member of the reigning family. When Pauline, soon after her return from the West Indies, bought this early-eighteenth-century house from the heirs of the Duc de Charost she hardly had the means to keep up, let alone modernise, so large a mansion. The agreed purchase price was 400,000 francs. Napoleon had contributed 300,000 francs, but she had been obliged to borrow the remaining 100,000 francs from Joseph and to negotiate a mortgage for 240,000 francs with her sister Elisa to pay for repairs and alterations.[1] The final payment to the Duchesse de Charost was not made till August 1805.

[1] The parity between the franc and the pound sterling from 1800 to 1914 was 25 francs = £1. Thus 1 franc 1800 was worth a little less than 10d. 1800, and the 400,000 francs which Pauline Bonaparte paid for the Hôtel de Charost in 1803 was the equivalent of £16,000 at that time. To provide the 800,000 francs for the purchase of the house and some of the contents in 1814 cost the British Government £32,000.

It is virtually impossible to calculate the relationship between the Napoleonic franc and the present-day franc in terms of real value, i.e. purchasing power. This is partly because the cost scale of basic commodities is no longer the same. Property values in particular are much higher to-day than they were in the early nineteenth century, i.e. a house could be bought for relatively less then than now. As a rough guide the new franc introduced by Napoleon in 1800 (the *franc Germinal* which replaced the *livre*) was worth about four times as much as the new franc introduced by General de Gaulle in 1963. Thus to Pauline Bonaparte 1 franc was worth 4 francs 1963, i.e. at the present franc-sterling rate of exchange about 6s.

The question is further complicated by changes in modern times in the franc-sterling parity. The present rate of exchange makes sterling worth not one-fourth but about one-seventh of the 1800 value in terms of the franc. For what it is worth, the 400,000 francs Pauline Bonaparte paid in 1803 and the 800,000 francs she received in 1814 for the Hôtel de Charost represent about £112,000 and £224,000 today.

Subject to the qualifications mentioned, the following rough and ready reckoner may help visualise the values of the sums in Napoleonic currency quoted in this book:

25 francs 1800 = £1 1800 = £7 1964;
1 franc 1800 = 10d. 1800 = 6s. 1964;
100 francs 1800 = £4 1800 = £28 1964.

At first she spent only comparatively small sums on repairs (12,000 francs) and new decorations (33,568 francs). The settlement of 1806 enabled her to be more enterprising. She employed the Bonaparte architects Percier and Fontaine, and furniture-makers like Jacob who were translating the achievements and the stamp of Napoleon's personality into the style which has left an enduring mark on history. The style of the First Empire, to Pauline, was a cult as well as a fashion.

The great house she had acquired was one of a series built in the newly fashionable Faubourg St. Honoré at the beginning of the eighteenth century and typical of the period—large, elegant, well-proportioned. The buildings, six or seven of them, were of a size, all had large gardens of the same dimensions, and, abutting on one another, formed a majestic row of grand mansions. Each consisted of a large central block set back from the street, flanked by a lodge on either side, one containing the kitchens, the other the stables. Over the kitchens of the Hôtel de Charost, to ensure instant identification, there is a sculpted pair of boars, over the stables a corresponding pair of horses' heads. A gateway with huge gates gave entrance from the street into a large and harmonious courtyard, separating the living quarters of the house from the noise of a busy thoroughfare.

Pauline did little to disturb the pleasing proportions of the splendid entrance to her Paris home, apart from improving the stables and carriage houses and enlarging the kitchens. But the house itself was not spacious enough in spite of the double range of lofty rooms on the ground and first floors. She added two great rooms on the garden front, one, on the west, to house Borghese's pictures and sculptures, the other, on the east, to serve as a state dining-room. Pauline herself lived on the first floor and used the enlarged ground floor for her dinners, balls and receptions. The new rooms were not paid for till 1809, when Napoleon settled her debts and gave her a more generous allowance. After her relations with Camillo became hopelessly strained, she came to a strictly business arrangement with him and charged him for his lodging and food on his visits to her house in Paris. On these rare occasions she gave him the first floor, moving to the ground floor herself. She used to complain of the noise of his footsteps over her head.

In great French eighteenth-century town houses everything was sacrificed to the splendour of the reception rooms. There were no corridors, apart from an occasional dark and tortuous passage cut between walls to allow servants access to their master's or mistress's apartments. Each room led into the next, and each, apart from those at the ends of the house, was therefore a passage. It was the same in the royal palaces. This inconvenient architectural arrangement had given rise to a set ceremonial, designed to protect as far as possible the privacy of the royal inhabitant. The lay-out of the Hôtel de Charost lent itself perfectly to the etiquette of a Napoleonic court. On mounting the grand staircase the visitor came to an ante-room on the courtyard side, where he waited or was if necessary interrogated by the Princess's staff. He then moved into another ante-room, on the garden side, where he probably found acquaintances also waiting their turn. The next salon, in the centre of the house and looking down the length of the garden, was where the Princess received visitors formally—the present *salon blanc et or*. Beyond that was the then *salon violet*, so called from the colour of the silk hangings with which the wall was covered (nowadays as in the time of the last Duc de Charost hung in green silk and called the *salon vert*). Here Pauline held her morning levée and during the rest of the day saw her intimates. Another room lay beyond the *salon violet*—Pauline's bedroom—at the end of the range of rooms.

Despite Napoleon's attempts to reduce court ceremonial to a minimum, the Bonapartes maintained the tradition of the levée, the occasion on which the royal personage held a reception in a state bedroom—a convenient way of enabling the prince or princess to meet courtiers and others admitted to the presence. A *lit de parade*, a splendid bed, not the bed in which the personage actually slept, was used for this ceremonial purpose. Pauline's bed is still on the first floor of the Hôtel de Charost. The highly elaborate, carved and gilded frame is supported at each corner by an Egyptian caryatid surmounted by a couchant leopard, and decorated in a riot of Napoleonic designs—arabesques, lyres and caducei, ivy-tendrils and laurel leaves. From a golden baldachin attached to the ceiling curtains of heavy damask fall around the bed. Over the baldachin she placed a golden eagle, Napoleon's eagle.

Her real bed was surprisingly simple—a little, low *lit de poupée* with muslin bed-curtains lined with rose-coloured material, as a young man admitted to the privacy of Pauline's bedroom described it in 1810. What struck this visitor most was the adjoining bathroom. It is next to the bedroom, a small room with a low ceiling. The bath is let into an alcove, in the style of the bathrooms in other Napoleonic residences. Pauline had a mania for baths—beyond the general family predilection. She liked to have a bath in milk, for the sake of her health as she herself made out, or perhaps for the sake of her complexion and the texture of her skin. But milk leaves a disagreeable odour; so the negro Paul, after he had prepared the Princess's bath, hurried up a back staircase which lies on the courtyard side of the house, went down a passage to a small room above the bath, and through an aperture constructed for the purpose poured down clear water—a primitive form of shower under which the milk was washed off the bather below.

When Pauline acquired it, the decoration of the house was that of the eighteenth century. In the hands of her architects and decorators it became a small palace in the latest style of the Empire. The carved, inviting chairs and settees of Louis XV and Louis XVI were replaced by the severe furniture of the Empire with its echoes of Bonaparte's conquests in the Orient. Gilded sphinxes were everywhere—over the lintels of the doors, supporting the arms of chairs and *canapés*. As a compliment to her brother she arranged for the star of the Legion of Honour, the new Order introduced by Napoleon in 1802, to be cunningly inserted in the capitals of eighteenth-century Corinthian columns. The austere, highly polished mahogany or marble of the Empire glittered in tables and *guéridons*. One such table, used for the game of *bouillotte*, still bears in faded ink the parchment heart-shaped label "Made for the Princess Pauline Bonaparte". A huge full-length looking-glass in a mahogany frame ornamented with the Napoleonic bee still stands in Pauline's bedroom. It was made for Napoleon with glass designed to diminish his corpulence. Pauline liked it and prevailed on him to give it to her. But much of the eighteenth century was left undisturbed—the chandeliers, the pilasters and many of the friezes with their grave mythological stories. If a little fresh and brash with its obelisks and sphinxes, it must have been a beautiful house then as now.

Like most of the Bonapartes, Pauline had a sense of style, though she followed rather than led the fashion: the best furniture was acquired from Murat. She also had her share of the family vitality, though it was increasingly lowered by ill-health. She entered with zest into the movement of the new age, and though she preferred to receive her intimates in small gatherings on the first floor of the Hôtel de Charost, she took pride in the large receptions she gave from time to time in the state salons on the ground floor. The first floor, with its more secluded rooms, was for her friends; the ground floor for official and fashionable Paris. Pauline, dressed in the severely classical style she helped to popularize, sat, or more often than not reclined, on a mahogany settee decorated with gilded lotus and laurel leaves, sphinxes and griffins, ready to greet her guests. The salon she preferred was the central room with gilded Ionic columns—the *salon d'honneur*—into which the guests passed after crossing the great entrance hall and a large ante-room. After they had paid their respects to the Princess they walked through two more salons into Pauline's new picture gallery, where in the course of the evening there was music, or crossed to the opposite wing where a great ormolu *surtout de table* glowed on a long supper table. All the rooms were bathed in the soft light of innumerable candles in gilded candelabra. On warm summer evenings the guests walked through the opened french windows across the garden court on to the lawns and through the shrubberies which stretched down to the Champs-Élysées.

When the last of the carriages had circled the courtyard and turned into the Faubourg, Pauline, with relief, walked up the grand staircase and found her way to the quiet room where her maids were waiting to help her undress and sink into her little muslin-curtained bed.

11. Mon bon petit frère
1805-7

EIGHTEEN HUNDRED AND FIVE—AS THE NEW YEAR OPENED
Pauline, had she ever reflected at all, would have concluded that
she was a fortunate young woman. Favourite sister of the
Emperor of the French, she enjoyed the prestige of that position.
As a member of the Imperial Family she was at the pinnacle of
French society. She could live in one of Marie Antoinette's
palaces when she was bored with her own house. She had her
own court and sufficient money to satisfy any reasonable whim.
What a vertiginous change from the obscurity and penury of
ten years ago! But it is doubtful whether Pauline ever reflected
on these things, any more than she rose to the surge and swing
of the new France which her brother had created or sensed the
imminence of the future great strokes of empire which were in
preparation. Pauline at twenty-four was bored, discontented
and out of sorts this New Year's Day.

Camillo, too, was unhappy and embarrassed. His marriage,
he recognised, was a failure. He was a fish out of water in the
glittering crystal bowl of the new French Empire: a husband
only in name, consort of a French princess for whom he no longer
had any respect or affection. His ambiguous position was
becoming intolerable. He had a strong homing instinct. He
wanted to go back to Italy. His francophilia, tested in the
crucible of life with the capricious sister of the Emperor of the
French, had evaporated. Prince Borghese's mood for once
became quite aggressive. He threatened to pack up and return
to Italy.

This state of affairs was reported to Napoleon. French
interests required the maintenance of the outward semblance at

least of this Imperial alliance. Borghese was given the Grand Cross of the Legion of Honour. A few weeks later he was made a French citizen, and shortly afterwards an Imperial Highness in his own right. Camillo could feel that he was no longer simply the *mari de madame*.

This did not suit Pauline at all. She did not want Camillo anywhere near her; she wanted him well out of sight. It was insufferably boring to have him following her from the Petit Trianon to St. Cloud, from St. Cloud to the Faubourg St. Honoré. Camillo must be sent away, as far away from Paris as possible. But even if she succeeded in goading him to leave Paris, she knew that Napoleon would order him back. Napoleon always insisted on the appearance of a happy and united ménage. She must speak to her brother and somehow persuade him. But Napoleon nowadays rarely had time to see her. At last, in June, he came to visit her at St. Cloud. To her joy he consented to find employment for Camillo away from Paris. He was forth-with appointed to command a squadron of horse grenadiers in the invasion army, and sent to Boulogne. Camillo himself was delighted. Pauline's health was miraculously restored. By early October she felt well enough to take up residence in the Hôtel de Charost.

Camillo soon had the opportunity to put further kilometres between himself and his wife. By the end of August the invasion forces assembled at the Channel ports were moving down to Strasbourg to regroup for action against the Austrians and Russians. Borghese volunteered to go with them.

Nobody had expected the uneasy lull to be durable. Napoleon was outspoken about his intentions to make more expansionist moves when he was ready. The threat of invasion openly mounted across the Channel was intolerable to the British. The Austrians, smarting from past defeats, were thirsting for revenge. The Russians were alarmed. The three govern-ments—British, Austrian and Russian—agreed that they must save themselves by forestalling Napoleon.

When in August 1805 the Austrians and Russians began

moving troops towards the French frontier, Napoleon did not hesitate. The plans for the invasion of England were called off and Napoleon aimed for the heart of Germany. The movement from Boulogne began on August 27. The Army of England became the Grand Army, and covered five hundred miles in less than eight weeks. By October 14 the French were in Munich, whereas the Austrian general staff had calculated that the French could not reach the Danube valley before mid-December. Napoleon himself remained in Paris while this movement of forces was proceeding, in order to deceive the enemy. It was not until September 23 that he left St. Cloud for the front. After desultory fighting, in which the Austrians under Mack were consistently defeated, he persuaded Mack to sur-render at Ulm. This, he knew, was only the first stage in the campaign. There remained the Russians—and the English. Napoleon habitually prepared his armies, and the French people, for struggles to come by means of proclamations addressed to the troops. It was an effective way of rallying public opinion to his policies and stimulating the morale of his troops.

"Soldiers of the Grand Army!" he wrote, "in fifteen days we have finished a campaign. Our intentions have been carried out: we have driven the troops of the House of Austria from Bavaria . . . But what cares England for that! Her object has been gained: we are no longer at Boulogne.

"Soldiers! this success is due to your unlimited confidence in your Emperor . . . But we cannot rest yet. You are impatient for a second campaign. The Russian army, drawn by the gold of England from the furthest limits of the earth, must suffer the same fate [as the Austrians]." The Grand Army now embarked on the long march eastwards to Vienna, thence northwards into Moravia, which was to bring the Russians and the depleted forces of their Austrian allies to battle at Austerlitz, near Brünn.

The Austrians had surrendered at Ulm on October 20. The next day Napoleon issued his proclamation to the troops, and on the same day the French fleet was defeated at Trafalgar. The news did not reach Napoleon until nearly three weeks later as he was pressing on from Ulm towards the river Inn. Méneval, who was with him, has recorded the shattering effect of this catastrophe which "postponed indefinitely all hope of destroying the English fleet". The Emperor, he says, felt that the only recourse left to him was the execution of a vast Continental blockade of England. Napoleon, in fact, as far back as 1798 had visualised that there were three ways of bringing the English to their knees: a direct invasion, for which the destruction of the English fleet was a prerequisite; the undermining of the English position in the Middle East and India; or French control of Northern Germany and the stoppage of British trade with Europe. The first had failed. The second had been tried once and foiled by the same English admiral at the Battle of the Nile. It might be tried again later, but clearly must be put aside for the present. There remained the third—the Continental Blockade.

Vienna surrendered without a blow, and after two satisfying days in the Imperial château of Schoenbrunn, Napoleon pressed northwards into Moravia and established his headquarters at the provincial capital, Brünn. After a personal reconnaissance he had selected a site near the village of Austerlitz as the best terrain, low hills declining to an open plain, for the desperate battle he expected to fight against superior forces. Even so, three days before the battle he was full of anxieties which he confided in a letter to Talleyrand. He was in fact in a terrible dilemma. If he fought it would be against heavy odds. If he delayed he risked finding the Germans, who were on the point of declaring war, encircling him from the rear. Like many another commander he revived his spirits by direct contact with his troops, and during the night before the battle toured the bivouacs on foot. The enthusiasm was indescribable. The men saluted him with cheers and waved improvised torches made of straw from their bedding. Méneval, who has recorded this scene, adds that, after early mist, "the sun shone the next morning on the battle of Austerlitz". It was perhaps Napoleon's most spectacular feat of arms. The Russo-Austrian army was cut in two. The Russian and

Austrian Emperors fled into the night. Peace terms were concluded at Pressburg (Bratislava) on December 26. Napoleon drove a hard bargain, consolidating the French positions in Italy and Germany at the expense of the Austrian Empire. The Austrians signed with bitterness and resentment.

Early in the new year of 1806 Napoleon was back in Paris. Great festivities were planned to celebrate the victory. Camillo, who had played an honourable if undistinguished rôle in the campaign, hurried back to take part. Pauline, dismayed at the prospect of her husband's return, made herself so disagreeable that Camillo changed his plans and decided to have his triumph in Rome. Decidedly, matters were going very badly between Pauline and Camillo. She by this time could scarcely bear to live in the same city with him. For his part Camillo was only too pleased to have any excuse to live in Italy.

As a result of the Peace of Pressburg Napoleon had in effect supplanted the Habsburgs, and, a new Holy Roman Emperor, disposed of various subject kingdoms and principalities. Wherever possible he liked to fill the available thrones with members of the family. Here at last was Pauline's chance. To her surprise she learnt that by a decree of March 30 she had been created Duchess of Guastalla. She was intrigued but had never heard of the place. Guastalla was in fact a principality in northern Italy which had been ceded to France along with the Duchies of Parma and Piacenza. "The principality of Guastalla being at our disposition," read the decree, "we do hereby dispose of it in favour of our well-beloved sister Pauline to enjoy it in full ownership and sovereignty under the titles of Princess and Duchess of Guastalla." This sounded impressive but Pauline was not satisfied. Caroline was Grand Duchess of Berg and Cleves, Elisa reigning Princess of Lucca; Joseph had become King of Naples, Louis, King of Holland. Neither Caroline nor Elisa was content, but Pauline was the most discontented of all. "It was a chorus of grievances," said Madame Junot, and Napoleon was provoked into commenting: "Will these ladies never be content? One would think we were really sharing the inheritance of the late king our father!" The Bonapartes were like any Corsican family when it came to a sharing-out of money and honours. Screams and scratches were the order of the day if favouritism was suspected. Pauline determined to have the matter out with Napoleon.

"What is Guastalla, *mon bon petit frère*?" she opened, ominously quiet. "Is it a fine big city, with a palace, with subjects and all?"

"It is a village," replied Napoleon tersely. Glancing at his sister, he hastily corrected himself: "A town, a borough in the states of Parma and Piacenza."

"A village, a town!" wailed Pauline. "And what do you expect me to do with it?"

"What you please," replied the embarrassed Emperor.

Pauline burst into tears; then, suddenly fierce and determined, rounded on her brother and said: "Napoleon, I swear I will tear your eyes out if you do not do better for me!"

The result was that Napoleon, perhaps contrite because Pauline had been worse treated than her two sisters, made an arrangement under which, while renouncing the duchy but retaining the title, Pauline received a guaranteed income considerably in excess of the revenues of the duchy. Once more Pauline had shown that, when it was an important matter of money or position, she could prevail over her impervious brother.

Pauline for all her youth—she was still only twenty-six—and in spite of the relatively quiet life she she had been leading, was in poor health. Whether she was aware of it or not, she was succuming gradually to the undermining of her health which was to bring her to an early grave. This summer of 1806 she felt sufficiently out-of-sorts to determine to take definite steps to cure herself, and decided to go and take the waters at Plombières in the Vosges. This set the pattern for many pilgrimages to watering-places all over Europe. It was also the first fatal step on a course in which the search for health and human affection became disastrously confused.

A journey for Pauline was a kind of escapade. She liked to tease and see the people about her being put to extraordinary trouble to satisfy her whims and caprices. Always fearful of being bored, she found a release in the ludicrous incidents she created round her. She was, of course, spoilt and pampered. Her position obliged her entourage to humour her. The journey from Paris to Plombières provided her with a golden opportunity to obtain this sort of special enjoyment. One of the stopping-places on the road to the Vosges was Bar-le-Duc, where she was to stay overnight with the Prefect. The Prefect was, in fact, her ex-brother-in-law, the elder brother of General Leclerc. Leclerc the Prefect knew of Pauline's fondness for baths and had been warned that she would want to have a bath in milk as soon as she arrived. He went to great pains to collect a sufficient quantity of milk. When Pauline and her considerable baggage-train drew up at the Prefecture he espied the bath with which she always travelled. Almost before he greeted his sister-in-law he ordered the bath to be placed in a salon and filled from the waiting milk pails. With satisfaction he bent low before Pauline and carried her gallantly and confidently into his house.

"I should like to have my bath," said Pauline.

"Certainly," said the Prefect. "It is ready."

"But where is the shower?" exclaimed Pauline, looking round the large salon where the bath filled with milk was placed. "My health requires a water shower after my bath in milk."

"I have no shower apparatus," muttered Leclerc.

"That is quite easy," she replied. "Just make a hole in the ceiling over the bath." And this is what was done.

Pauline continued her journey to Plombières, and there she found Auguste de Forbin and the first overwhelming emotional experience of her adult life.

Comte Louis Nicholas Philippe Auguste de Forbin, descendant of an ancient Provençal family, was twenty-nine when he and Pauline met on a wet summer's day at Plombières. His family, like many others, had been ruined during the Revolution and after his father's death during the Terror Auguste drifted to Paris, not to seek his fortune but to study painting under Granet and David. Conscripted into the army, he had seen active service in 1799 and in the victorious Austrian campaign of 1800.

Forbin was a dilettante. Bored with the army, he painted a little, wrote a little, talked amusingly. Tall and distinguished in appearance, with regular features and fine eyes, he had a certain air of the *ancien régime*. Lively and intelligent, he was, to the discerning eye of Madame Junot, "an accomplished gentleman" and women were mad about him. Pauline fell deeply and passionately in love for the first time. Forbin's emotions were not so deeply engaged, but he liked her well enough, or found it sufficiently amusing to be the lover of the Emperor's sister, to consent to follow her to Paris. The unsuspecting Napoleon agreed to appoint Forbin Chamberlain of Princess Pauline's household.

That winter of 1806 everybody commented on the beauty and high spirits of Pauline. She was delighted to play her part in affairs of State and receive Paris society on behalf of the Emperor, in the absence of Joséphine who had joined him in Germany during the campaign against the Prussians. Once again Madame Junot has pictured the scene. "The Princess's entry into the drawing-room was really breath-taking, so beautiful was she. She was wearing a dress of rose-coloured tulle lined with satin of the same colour decorated with marabou feathers held in place by diamond brooches." Pauline was radiantly happy. But this state of affairs did not last. Once again her health broke down, not this time from boredom but because her constitution could not stand the delirium of her new-found happiness. Dr. Peyre became seriously alarmed and, knowing that Pauline never listened to his advice, persuaded her to be examined by Hallé, the most celebrated gynæcologist of the day. Hallé sent Peyre a long report (first published in 1893 by Arthur Lévy in *Napoléon Intime* and subsequently quoted by many of Pauline's biographers). The specialist took a very serious view of her condition, which he diagnosed as a chronic inflammation of the womb accompanied by general prostration and exhaustion. Proposing no specific remedy, he advised strongly that Pauline must mend her ways and lead a quiet life. In veiled language he indicated that he had her love-affair with Forbin in mind. With his experience of the Court, he understood the temptations to which this "pretty, impressionable young woman living alone" was exposed. He knew the unsatisfactory state of her marriage to Borghese. He divined her passionate nature, yet passion was the one indulgence her state of health would not allow. As a psychologist, he recognised the interaction of the physical and the psychological sides of her condition. He saw with clarity that Pauline had reached a dangerous crisis.

"We must save this young and interesting woman from ruin," he concluded, urging that it was Peyre's duty to break up the liaison "if there is anyone who is taking advantage of her weaknesses and abetting them"—a clear pointer to Forbin.

Pauline's health has inevitably been a subject of interest to her biographers because it loomed so large in her way of life and also in her technique of living. There is nothing to suggest that in youth she was anything but a normally healthy, if unusually high-spirited, young woman. The birth of Dermid in 1798 was attended by post-natal complications, and though no details are recorded, it seems possible, in view of Hallé's diagnosis nine years later, that the origins of her malady are to be found in that youthful ordeal. She was ill when she returned from San Domingo at the age of twenty-two, but is not known to have contracted any serious disease. It was in the summer of 1804, when she was twenty-three, that she first started to visit cure-places, drink the waters and take medicinal baths. Though medical details once again are lacking, this suggests that she was suffering from an internal ailment. Her predilection for reposing for hours on a chaise-longue (beyond the requirements of the prevailing fashion), her habit of being carried in a sedan-chair, when travelling, to mitigate the distress she felt in riding in a carriage on long journeys—all indicate that she was subject to some kind of internal discomfort. There are no details of her final illness. She herself, towards the end of her life, said that, like Napoleon, it was her liver that was killing her. The nature of Pauline's malady must remain in doubt because the contemporary records are imprecise. It was not the custom in her day to reveal such details; women, on the contrary, kept their medical secrets to themselves. However, it is difficult to resist the conclusion that her death at the early age of forty-four was due to cancer, as has been suggested by some of her biographers.

If the seeds of her premature end were implanted after childbirth, when she was only seventeen, this, of course, was not known to the wilful, pleasure-loving, temperamental Pauline. Her temperament hastened her end. Her state of health, indeed, may have acted as an irritant to her naturally passionate nature and thus, in a vicious circle, have contributed to the gradual undermining of health and morale. Shattered by the loss of her son, frustrated in her married life with Borghese, exposed by her position as Napoleon's sister to flattery and adulation, she gave way too easily to extravagances which her state of health should never have permitted.

The Family, Napoleon and Madame Mère in particular, were inclined to discount the ups-and-downs of Pauline's health. This was partly her fault, since she frequently "made herself ill" in order to establish a pretext for leaving some place she disliked or to work on the feelings of Napoleon. On this occasion, however, her mother was seriously alarmed. Hallé wrote his report on April 22, 1807. Armed with the report, Peyre spoke to Madame Mère. The Signora spoke severely to her daughter. Before she could persuade her to stop seeing Forbin, she had to threaten to reveal the liaison to Napoleon, who would certainly order Forbin to rejoin his regiment. Pauline finally agreed to see Forbin no more and to have a thorough cure at Aix-les-Bains. On the way she visited her Uncle Fesch at Lyons. She promised him never to see Forbin again. She had one fleeting encounter with him at Aix, but was too ill and too demoralised to resist the army of doctors who now insisted that she should move to Gréoux-les-Bains, a small watering-place in the Basses-Alpes, some thirty miles to the east of Aix-en-Provence. From there she wrote letter after letter to Forbin. They are curiously reminiscent of her despairing letters to Fréron. Pauline at twenty-seven was the same restless, capricious creature, full of complaints and self-pity, as the Paulette of seventeen. Why could she and Forbin not have been left in peace? It was Peyre who had given them away, "not out of unkindness," wrote Pauline on June 10, "but because he is a coward and a fool. Mama and my uncle know everything, and you cannot imagine what I went through at Lyons." She complained of the members of her household, who had all in varying degrees betrayed her. "So I only see Minette, Emilie and Nini"—her three maids. She ended, as she always tended to close this kind of letter, in Italian. "*Ti mando dei fiori che sono stati nel mio seno, li ho coperto di baci.*—I send you some flowers, covered in kisses, which have lain in my bosom."

It sounded like the end, and perhaps Pauline was genuinely resigned to renouncing Forbin. But the cure at Gréoux was doing her good, and by September she had regained her spirits. On the spur of the moment she decided she had had enough of this dull little town and announced her intention of going to Aix-en-Provence. There was no time for her cumbersome household to pack up, and she set forth with one or two attendants only. At Aix-en-Provence, at La Mignarde, she set up a miniature court, and the first person she summoned was Forbin. But Forbin had changed. He was no more his docile self, often he was positively irritating. Once she threw a book at him. Forbin did not take long to make his decision. This ailing, capricious woman no longer interested him, and he was nervous about his personal position now that Camillo, back from the Prussian campaign, had arrived at La Mignarde. Napoleon, a stickler for the outward appearances of decorum in the lives of members of the Imperial Family, would be capable of packing him off abroad on some dangerous or unhealthy mission. In October Forbin hurriedly left Aix-en-Provence and headed north. At Fontainebleau he asked the Emperor's permission to see active service. Napoleon agreed on the spot and appointed him to a post in the garrison in the Gironde. Bordeaux was a far cry from Paris or Provence.

During the next two years Forbin saw service in the campaigns of Portugal, Spain and Austria, retired honourably from the army in 1809, and was made a Baron of the Empire. He had to await the fall of the Empire for the artistic and literary side of his character to find its full development. Under the Restoration he was appointed a director of museums, reorganised the Louvre and created several new galleries, including one for the work of contemporary artists, travelled widely in the Levant and Egypt, and, besides writing books on art and travel, became an established painter of landscapes and architectural subjects. His full life—he died at the age of seventy-four in 1841—was marked, like that of most of his contemporaries, by the political upheavals of his time. An aristocrat by origin, an artist by temperament, he was swept into revolution and war, and—what was worse for him—into the inner circle of the Bonapartes. He had to wait for middle age and the more tranquil days of the Restoration for his true bent to come to fruition. But he will be remembered, not as a landscape artist or a museum director, but as the elegant thirty-year-old dilettante who was loved by Pauline Borghese.

III

Mists in Idleness

12. The Best Moment
1806–7

AT THE TIME OF FORBIN'S APPEARANCE AT FONTAINE-
BLEAU in the autumn of 1807, Napoleon had recently returned
from a campaign in which he had driven victoriously into
Prussia and Poland and in a series of staggering military triumphs
defeated the Prussians and the Russians. The previous year there
had seemed to be some hope of negotiating a peaceful settlement in Europe. Pitt had died on January 23, 1806, and was
succeeded by Fox, for long an advocate of peace with France. In
the absence of diplomatic relations between the countries, Fox
arranged for the Earl of Yarmouth, one of the many Englishmen
under restraint in Paris, to enter into discussions with Talleyrand.
With the help of the Earl of Lauderdale, who replaced him in
the final stages of the discussions, Yarmouth and the French
negotiators worked away patiently during the spring and summer.
By September, when Fox was on his death-bed, it was clear
that no settlement was possible. The Russians were threatening
war; the Prussians were not prepared to rise to the bait of
Hanover, the English King's possession which Napoleon had
seized after the rupture with England in 1803 and which he
now offered to King Frederick William; and the British were
improving their position overseas. On October 8, the Prussian
envoy in Paris presented an ultimatum, including a request for
the withdrawal of French troops from southern Germany. This
brought matters to a head. Lauderdale, who had stayed on for
three weeks after the death of Fox on September 13, had had
his final interview on October 6. Napoleon had left Paris twelve
days before to marshal his troops for the inevitable offensive.
"It is really quite amusing," commented Napoleon, "that the

Prussians should have handed me their ultimatum on the 8th; and that I, without knowing this, should have entered Bayreuth and begun my movements on the 7th."

None of these manœuvrings for position, none of these preparations for great events, affected Pauline as she organised her Paris house and wandered from one watering-place to another in search of health and distraction. Placed by birth and chance in the inmost circle of the greatest conqueror of modern times, she was uninterested in political affairs, or in obtaining the power and influence over events and people which were hers for the asking. But she was a Bonaparte and needed outlets for her share of the family brilliance and energy. Her nature prevented her from finding scope in political intrigue. Nobody would have been surprised if she had done that. Indeed, she was blamed because she did not. Yet it is hard to criticise this little Corsican, who found herself swept up into a maelstrom of events for which she did not care and which she did not understand.

Pauline had been living in the Hôtel de Charost, completely absorbed by Forbin, when Napoleon crushed the Prussians on October 14, 1806, in the twin battles of Jena and Auerstadt. On October 27 the French armies entered Berlin. Joséphine had joined Napoleon in Germany during the winter, and it was then that Pauline presided at one or two receptions on behalf of the Emperor. But it is doubtful whether, on these occasions, conversation with her guests touched on European events or indeed whether she thought of these formal receptions as anything except occasions for her to appear in a magnificent new robe and dazzle Paris society.

In the spring of 1807, while Pauline lay seriously ill at Aix-les-Bains, Napoleon was deep in Poland, waiting for the thaw which would enable the French armies to move against the Russians. When, on June 14, Napoleon utterly defeated Bennigsen at Friedland, Pauline was at Gréoux, alone with the household officials and ladies-in-waiting whom she detested, longing for Forbin, ill and bored. For all her lack of comprehension of the tremendous events taking place in Eastern Europe, Pauline knew her brother to be a very great man, a conqueror comparable to Alexander the Great. She could certainly understand the drama of the meeting which took place on June 25, 1807, near Tilsit, between the Emperor of the French and the Tsar of All the Russias. After the defeat of Friedland, Alexander had made overtures for peace and the result was this meeting between the two Emperors on a raft moored in mid-stream on the river Niemen, which formed the limit of the French advance. "It was a beautiful sight," wrote Méneval, who was present. "The two sovereigns with a spontaneous movement fell into each other's arms and embraced." The armies, or rather the survivors of the armies, ranged on the banks of the river, cheered vociferously, and the two rulers got down to work. Behind the panoply of sabres and soldiery, the chivalry symbolised by the neutral meeting-place in mid-stream, the romance surrounding the confrontation of the two rulers of Europe, lay the hard calculating mind of the man who had made himself master of Western Europe and the impressionable idealism of the hereditary autocrat of the Russian empire.

Napoleon was clear on his objectives. They were simple. In return for the reduction of Prussia to second-class status and help in pursuing the war against Great Britain, he was prepared to share the hegemony of Europe with Russia and conclude an alliance. Napoleon exerted all his charm. The Tsar appeared to be captivated by the personality of the dynamic self-made little man in whom he recognised the greatest captain of the age. Napoleon recorded, after their first meeting on the raft: "I am very pleased with him; he is a handsome and excellent young Emperor, and has more intelligence than is generally supposed." The two autocrats became inseparable. They went and lived in Tilsit, in separate establishments, in the same street. They spent nearly three weeks together, seeing each other all day long. Since the Tsar spoke perfect French, they could converse freely without interpreters. They used daily to ride out together, visiting their troops, holding reviews and eating with the rank and file. They were enchanted with each other; or rather, the self-made ruler of a decade enchanted the autocrat of centuries. "So intimate did the two Emperors become," noted Méneval, "that when on returning from their excursions the Tsar was to dine with Napoleon, the latter would not allow him to go home to change his dress." Napoleon lent the excellent young Emperor his own cravats and placed his big gold travelling bag at his disposal. When Alexander commended the neatness of the bag and the quality of its fittings, Napoleon promptly made him a present of it.

This kind of gesture had its effect on the susceptible and trusting young Tsar, and Napoleon had little difficulty in achieving his objectives. Alexander pleaded for his friend and ally King Frederick William, but Napoleon was adamant in his determination to crush Prussia. (The two Emperors usually took the poor King of Prussia with them on their excursions; but they withdrew alone into a little gallery when they discussed business after dinner.) Napoleon also succeeded in persuading the Tsar to turn against his ancient ally, Great Britain. This was embarrassing for the Russians, and it was arranged to keep this part of the Tilsit agreement secret. The news leaked, and the London Government decided that instant action was needed to protect the country against a move by the two great Continental Empires. To keep open the mouth of the Baltic and maintain communications with Sweden, and to make sure that the Danish fleet did not fall into French or Russian hands, the English, in September 1807, sent an expedition to seize the Danish fleet at Copenhagen. (This unexpected stroke in its turn prompted a French counterstroke against Portugal, whose ports were open to British commerce. An expedition under General Junot seized Lisbon, and the Portuguese royal family fled to Brazil.)

In Paris Pauline, the Family, the new Imperial society and the ordinary Parisian basked in the refulgence of their Emperor's glory. The Franco-Russian alliance arranged at Tilsit, coming after the two spectacular campaigns which preceded it, struck the French of the day as the greatest of Napoleon's military and diplomatic triumphs. "It lifted the power and the glory of the

Emperor Napoleon to their highest summits;" such was the opinion of Napoleon's secretary. Napoleon himself said at St. Helena that perhaps Tilsit was the best moment.

On July 7, 1807, at the conclusion of the Tilsit meeting, Napoleon wrote to Joséphine: "I have just concluded peace. People tell me I am wrong and that I shall be taken in; but, faith, we have made enough war and must give the world repose." On the 9th: "The Emperor Alexander and I parted today after spending twenty days together here. We gave one another tokens of the greatest friendship." On the 18th he spent the night at Dresden with the King of Saxony and, in the playful mood which came over him when his affairs were prospering, wrote to Joséphine: "I am now halfway back to you. One of these fine nights I shall turn up at St. Cloud like a jealous husband; be warned." On July 27, 1807, at 5 a.m., he was back at the château, after ten months away from Paris.

13. Turin
1808

PAULINE SPENT THE AUTUMN AND WINTER OF 1807-8 IN
the south of France. With the coming of spring she was ready to
return to Paris. But once again her life was suddenly disrupted
by the political requirements of the Empire. She had recovered
health and spirits in the Midi. Though never happy when away
for long from the excitement and brilliance of Paris, she was still
a child of the Mediterranean. Always restless, she soon grew
tired of Aix-en-Provence and decided to return to Marseille,
scene of so many childhood memories. But the Marseillais,
never friendly to the Bonapartes, were far from welcoming.
What was worse, the old scandals about Pauline and her sisters
in the days of the Terror were raked up. There were plenty of
people in Marseille who still remembered that the daughters of
Madame Mère had earned a precarious livelihood as laundresses
and seamstresses. So by mid-October Pauline decided to move
further along the coast.

Near Nice, still in 1807 a little fishing-port, she installed herself in a magnificent villa belonging to a Monsieur Vinaille,
which the Prefect had requisitioned for the Emperor's sister.
Here she established a much more regular routine of life than
she cared to do in Paris, with set hours for meals with her household, morning visits from delegations of local notables, afternoon
excursions on the sea or into the countryside, and, before and
after dinner, musical evenings.

Music played an important part in the round of this miniature
court, for a reason, as often with Pauline, that was purely personal. She had found in Paris some months earlier a charming
Italian *chef d'orchestre*, whom she now engaged at a handsome
salary as a member of her household at Nice. Felix Biangini, a

year younger than Pauline, was twenty-six, a competent musician and a very timid young man. However hard-working a pupil, however enthusiastic a devotee of music, it was clear to him that the sudden interest of Pauline, who, a true Bonaparte, had no ear or voice, had been aroused by considerations not exclusively artistic. Biangini was thoroughly alarmed. The memoirs in which he recorded his stay at Pauline's court at the Villa Vinaille show that he was acutely conscious of the watchful eye of the Emperor and the fate that was liable to overtake the Princess's favourites. "I knew what had happened to Monsieur de Forbin and was quite aware that the Emperor was regularly informed what his sister did and whom she saw." In fact he need not have been so concerned. As the presence of his sister, at Pauline's invitation, should have shown, this was not one of her great romances. She simply thought it would be amusing to flirt mildly with a tame artist at hand to help while away the quiet provincial days in musical soirées. The winter passed agreeably for her. She felt much better and was looking forward to returning to Paris. Suddenly the blow fell. An Imperial courier arrived one evening in February 1808 at the Villa Vinaille. She read out to her household at dinner the instruction which brought to a close this pastoral interlude in the south of France.

"We have deemed it desirable," she read, "to appoint our brother-in-law to the dignity of Governor-General of the peoples of our departments beyond the Alps, who will thus recognise our desire to be more immediately informed of their interests and more closely in touch with the more distant parts of our Empire." What did Pauline care if Napoleon had decided to create a new "government-general beyond the Alps"? She had not the slightest desire to live in Turin, the capital of the new state as it had been of the Kingdom of Sardinia, which it replaced. She viewed with repulsion the prospect of living again with Borghese and appearing constantly with him in public with a forced smile on her face. For a moment she consoled herself with the thought that she would be a real princess, living in a real palace, with a real court and all that went with it in the way of attendants and guards, pomp and ceremony. Then, to her utter dismay, she learnt that all these appurtenances would be Camillo's, not hers. Camillo, the despised Camillo, would be the Governor-General, the one who gave the orders and dispensed the money. Yet in her heart of hearts she knew she would have to submit. In a way she was content to do so; she recognised that she was an element in her brother's Imperial plans. When it was Napoleon the Emperor speaking she obeyed. She waited with resignation for the arrival of Camillo.

Camillo eventually reached Nice from Paris on April 13, 1808, with an immense baggage-train and a considerable staff. Among them was Maxime de Villemarest, his private secretary, who recorded in great detail his impressions of Prince Borghese's mission. The night of their arrival the two staffs all had dinner together, while Camillo and Pauline dined alone. Villemarest, who had never seen Pauline, waited impatiently for the moment when the suite would be summoned to meet the Princess after dinner. He found the reality even more arresting than the report. She had an indescribable quality of ideal beauty, he wrote, fine features and a coquettish air. She was a *femme-femme*, than which, for Villemarest, there could be no higher praise. She looked languid and delicate, but the real life and force of her personality made itself felt. There was something of Napoleon in her expression. Villemarest, in a word, was stunned by Pauline, who certainly must have recovered her looks and her spirits as a result of the relatively calm and orderly life she had been leading for the past twelve months.

Five days later the court set off on the journey across the mountains northwards to Turin, with a long baggage-train containing trunk after trunk filled with the innumerable dresses Pauline had ordered from Leroy, Camillo's uniforms, and various dinner services of which the pieces had been carefully counted up by Napoleon's orders in Paris and assigned according to the needs of the post. Napoleon wished his brother-in-law to cut a good figure among the Piedmontese, but everything must be strictly inventoried.

The journey, of which Villemarest wrote a lively account, took five days. The road was rough and at times dangerous. The weather was tempestuous. Pauline was in a bad temper and complained incessantly. Everything possible was done for her comfort; when, for example, at particularly steep stretches of the road, the others left the heavy travelling-coaches and walked, Pauline was carried in a sedan-chair. The coach in which she travelled had been specially made by the best coach-maker in Paris and brought by Borghese from the capital. But nothing pleased Pauline from the start of the journey. It is likely that she felt ill and uncomfortable, as she often did. In her restless life she suffered innumerable hours of discomfort on the roads of France and Italy. Not only was this particular journey exceptionally arduous; journey's end was thoroughly unwelcome. She expressed her feelings by nagging and teasing Camillo, who seems to have handled her with commendable tact and patience. She felt ill on reaching the mountain village where they were to spend the first night, and since a special kind of veal broth was the only thing she could tolerate for dinner, she had the villagers and the entourage in an uproar until they could find a calf—in mountainous country where only sheep and goats were indigenous. At the next mountain village a deputation from Turin, the first of many, presented an address of welcome to the Governor-General. Pauline insisted on making a reply as well as Borghese. She was, she maintained, of higher rank than her husband.

From the moment they made their ceremonial entry into Turin on April 23, 1808, she realised that for once she would be obliged to play second fiddle to Camillo. The ceremonial in its smallest detail had been drawn up by Napoleon himself in such a way as to emphasise the position of the Governor-General. Pauline, reluctantly reconciling herself to the rôle of consort, sat on the Prince's left at official ceremonies. And how many ceremonies there were! It was a continuous round of audiences, courts, reviews, grand dinners and balls, with hardly an evening free for the small, intimate, informal parties that she loved.

Biangini was with her, but the etiquette of the Governor-General's court had no place for those delightful musical evenings of the past winter, replaced nowadays by long formal appearances at the opera house. Biangini, terrified of being compromised, and exiled, kept as far out of her sight as possible. Soon the inevitable psychosomatic cycle started again. Pauline fell ill. She *was* ill, or perhaps she made herself ill.

She wrote to Napoleon begging leave to visit the hot springs at Aosta. Lucien, who had been living in retirement in Rome since his break with Napoleon in 1807, came to see her. He told her about the terrible final scene with their brother. Napoleon had left Fontainebleau the previous November for a short tour in Italy to assure himself that all was well in the Italian dominions wrested from the Austrians and to satisfy himself that Joseph was managing matters satisfactorily in his kingdom of Naples. Napoleon was mistrustful of the Austrians. Another reason for undertaking this lightning journey was the prospect of a meeting with Lucien. The two brothers met at Mantua on December 13, 1807. They had not seen each other since the day of Austerlitz and talked from nine in the evening till midnight.

Napoleon urged him to accept a foreign throne and give up his wife, the former Madame Jouberton. A large map of Europe lay on the table. "Choose any kingdom you wish," said Napoleon. Lucien replied that he disapproved of the Empire; his republican convictions were unchanged. Napoleon roughly dismissed these Utopian ramblings. "I will make you the greatest man in Europe—next to myself," he added hastily. Lucien was unmoved. Yet when Napoleon, with the charm and conviction he knew how to deploy, appealed to his brotherly friendship, Lucien was shaken. In his heart of hearts he loved Napoleon. Turning pale, he said he would accept a kingdom if he was allowed to rule it according to his own notions. This infuriated Napoleon. The two brothers glared at each other across the map of Europe. After a long silence: "You will reflect," said the Emperor. "Night brings counsel. Goodbye, and a good night to you, my brother."

Lucien knew this was the end. He could not speak. He was torn between his sense of family, his respect for his brother in the position he now occupied, and his deepest, unshakeable convictions. When he left the room, he was in tears. He was not to see Napoleon again till 1815.

Fond as she was of Lucien, Pauline insisted on seeing him even though she had heard of the quarrel. But they met more or less clandestinely and she was glad to see him go, since she feared Napoleon would hear of their meeting and suspect an intrigue against himself. Pauline was normally without a trace of moral cowardice, and she must have been really low in health and spirits to give way to such timidity.

In May Joseph came to see her on his way from his capital in Naples to Bayonne, where he had been summoned to meet the Emperor. He had not seen Pauline for two years. As the eldest, who would have been head of the clan but for Napoleon's vertiginous rise to power, he was secretly critical of his brother. He and Pauline privately sympathised with Lucien, admired him for his tenacity in standing by his principles and his determination to keep his domestic happiness where he had found it. Pauline had not particularly wanted to marry an Italian prince; she envied Lucien his wayward Alexandrine. Joseph had not wanted to be a king. He liked literature and art, and the company of artists and learned men. He felt out of place as King of Naples, surrounded by pomp and protocol, spending his days in government and ceremonial, ever conscious of the overseeing eye of his tyrannical brother. He had a shrewd idea why Napoleon had summoned him to Bayonne and feared that he would be instructed to occupy some even more difficult and uncongenial throne. It was painful to be a brother of Napoleon if you were a king. A sovereign only in name, you were treated like a French prefect. He had told Napoleon long ago that he "preferred to reign at Mortefontaine".

As they talked with animation, brother and sister looked very much alike. They had the same strong features, the same mildness and intelligence of expression. Joseph was concerned at Pauline's changed appearance. Clearly she was really ill. None of the rest of the family, not even Madame Mère, took Pauline's ill-health seriously. Joseph, warm-hearted and compassionate, understood. This favourite sister was stricken in health and, what was worse, demoralised. Obviously she ought to leave Piedmont and go at once to one of the spas, Aix-les-Bains for example, which she knew and where she had a good chance of recovering. But this would mean defying Napoleon's edict that she was to stay at the Governor-General's side and not leave the territory of Piedmont without his permission. Joseph did what he could. Before resuming his journey to Bayonne he sent a letter ahead to Napoleon by express. "I have found Paulette in a deplorable state," he wrote. "She has not eaten for eight days and cannot keep even the lightest bouillon down. The doctors say she ought to leave the humid climate of Turin and go to Aix in Savoy."

Weeks passed, with no reply from Bayonne. She asked Villemarest to write and represent that Piedmont was killing her. At last a letter from the Emperor was delivered in Turin (it had taken five weeks for him to write an answer)—a cold, unsympathetic letter.

"I have received your letter of May 18. I approve your going to take the waters at the Val d'Aosta. I am sorry to learn your health is bad. I suppose you are behaving yourself, and that none of this is your own fault. I am happy to see you are pleased with your Piedmontese *dame d'honneur* and ladies. Make yourself liked. Be affable with everybody. Try to be equable, and keep the Prince happy."

Napoleon had not forgotten about Forbin and Dr. Peyre's report. A fortnight later he wrote another letter:

"You are merely suffering from the natural effects of spring weather. I see no objection to your going to the waters of Saint-Didier, since they are in the region of the Government-General. But you are not to leave the region without my authority."

Before these highly unhelpful messages had reached Turin,

Pauline had made up her mind. Napoleon did not understand that she was desperately ill, or, if he did, considered it more important for her to play her official rôle in this isolated corner of the French Empire. She defied her brother's wishes, left Piedmont and went to Aix-les-Bains, where she arrived on June 6. After five weeks she felt well enough to travel, and before the end of July 1808 was back in the Hôtel de Charost in Paris. Some might say, and several—among them Biangini and her sister Elisa—did say that Pauline's illness was a trumped-up affair to enable her to return to Paris and escape from the double duress of life in an Italian city and life with Camillo Borghese. But Joseph's report alone is evidence enough that Turin had reduced Pauline to an alarmingly low state of health. It had also reduced her to taking the uncongenial step of defying the Emperor. Never, in the ups-and-downs of their sister-brother, subject-sovereign relationship, had Pauline so desperately needed the sympathy of a brother. All she was vouchsafed was the cold judgment of a ruler. It was too much. She took matters into her own hands.

When in mid-May Joseph arrived at Pau, on the last stage of his journey to Bayonne, he found a letter from Napoleon. It informed him that he was to give up the Kingdom of Naples and assume the throne of Spain. The Spanish Government and the Bourbon dynasty had just signed Spain over to France. "In Madrid," said Napoleon, "you are in France. Naples is at the world's end."

This may or may not have been Joseph's first intimation of the project, but he was certainly appalled by the prospect. However, always ready to do what Napoleon asked, with deep misgiving he acquiesced. The throne of Naples was to be filled by Napoleon's brother-in-law Murat, Grand Duke of Berg, who had been commanding the French forces in Spain. Pauline thus learnt that one of her two sisters, Caroline, was to be a queen.

The events which led up to this fantastic *coup* for the Bonaparte family were a long and tortuous story of corruption and decadence on the Spanish side, of force and intrigue on the

French. It began when Napoleon decided to seize Portugal as a reprisal for the British attack on the Danish fleet in Copenhagen and to close Portuguese ports to British trade as part of the policy of starving out Britain by applying a continent-wide blockade of British commerce. Junot—much to his chagrin, according to his wife Laure—had been appointed to command the expedition soon after Napoleon returned to Paris in late July 1807 following his triumphal meeting with the Tsar at Tilsit. According to Madame Junot, his orders, written at Napoleon's dictation by Méneval, were succinct and to the point: "Enter Lisbon, and take possession of the shipping and dockyards." Junot was successful. The Portuguese royal family fled to Brazil, Portugal was in French hands.

With this toe-hold on the Iberian peninsula, Napoleon turned his attention towards Spain. Under the plea of keeping open Junot's communications with France, large numbers of troops were sent to Spain. By the early days of 1808 there were about 40,000 in Northern Spain and 12,000 in Catalonia, besides Junot's 20,000 in Portugal. On February 20, 1808, the Grand Duke of Berg had been appointed Supreme Commander of the French forces and the Emperor's Lieutenant in Spain.

The Spanish monarchy and government, as Napoleon knew, were in disarray. The King, Charles IV, a futile and ineffective potentate, had surrendered the reins of government to Godoy, the Prince of the Peace, a title gained at the time of the alliance concluded between Spain and post-revolutionary France in 1795. Godoy himself was the lover of the ambitious, head-strong queen. The scandalous relations between the Queen and the favourite had incensed the Prince of the Asturias, Ferdinand, heir to the throne. This unhealthy situation provided a wonderful opening for an adroit mixture of diplomacy and power politics. Napoleon ordered Murat to move on Madrid and keep talking.

"Continue your kindly talk," he instructed his lieutenant. "Reassure the King, the Prince of the Peace, the Prince of the Asturias, the Queen. The chief thing is to reach Madrid."

The Duke of Wellington
by Gérard. Painted in 1814
while he was British Ambassador
in Paris and now in the
British Embassy

Photo Z. Mihanoff, Paris

Marchand, Napoleon's valet
after 1814. Painter unknown

Photo Bulloz

Laure Junot, Duchesse d'Abrantès
Radio Times Hulton Picture Library

The Château of Neuilly, Pauline's second Paris home
Radio Times Hulton Picture Library

The news of Murat's advance on Madrid produced a panic at the royal palace at Aranjuez. The King, the Queen, Godoy— all were convinced that they were lost and that their only recourse was flight to the Americas. The unpleasant young Ferdinand saw his chance. He roused his supporters, denounced the favourite, raised a riot, and so alarmed his parents that Charles IV abdicated in his favour. This was on March 19, 1808. The young King entered Madrid to the acclaim of the populace delighted by the fall of the favourite, to find the city occupied by French troops. To his dismay, Murat was not disposed to recognise him as king.

This was exactly how Napoleon could have wished the hand to be played. He hurried down to Bayonne in early April and invited Charles IV and the Queen, Godoy, and Ferdinand to come there and talk matters over. All arrived by the end of April. By snubbing Ferdinand and playing up to the old King, Napoleon was able, on May 5, 1808, to conclude an agreement under which Charles IV agreed to hand over Spain and the Indies in return for castles in France and a pension. No doubt to Napoleon, immersed during all this time in bringing off a tremendous *coup de main*, the plaintive letters of his sister in far-away Italy must have seemed an irritating intrusion. A lesser man might have thought five weeks rather long to leave unanswered an insistent plea from a favourite sister.

This, or something very like it, must have been the account which Joseph was given when he arrived in Bayonne shortly after the May 5 agreement. It was with mixed feelings, after listening to this tale of duplicity and corruption, that he proceeded to Madrid to take charge of his new kingdom and preside over his new subjects, whose interests had counted for nothing and who were no willing parties to this whole murky transaction.

14. Neuilly
1808-9

IN PARIS ON AUGUST 15, 1808, THE FEAST OF THE ASSUMP-
tion, there was a banquet followed by a ball at the Hôtel de Ville.
The City of Paris was honouring the Emperor, who had hurried
back from Spain and reached St. Cloud the day before in order
to be present for the celebration of his birthday. A few days
later Pauline had a long talk with him—the first for nearly two
years. Napoleon had left Paris in October 1806 for the campaigns
against Prussia and Russia, and by the time he returned at the end
of July 1807, Pauline was moving from one health resort to
another and later went to Piedmont. It is not known exactly
what passed between brother and sister. Pauline must have been
resentful at his lack of consideration. Napoleon, perhaps, was
penitent. At all events, he was forgiving and promised to concern himself with her financial situation. She would, however,
have to wait till he returned from Germany. "He is leaving for
Germany," Pauline wrote to a friend, "on September 22 at
latest."

Napoleon did in fact leave Paris on that date and, travelling
hard as he always did, arrived on the 27th at Erfurt. There he
spent three weeks with the Tsar. The profound alarm which this
meeting stirred up in Europe and in England and the course of
events in Spain meant that several months were to elapse before
Napoleon could turn his mind to his little sister's money affairs.

The faithful Méneval, always at his master's side, has described
the splendour and outward cordiality of the meeting. Napoleon,
who considered Erfurt part of the French Empire, timed his
arrival so as to be there to receive the Tsar, whom he insisted, as
host, on entertaining to dinner every night. The Tsar was always

placed on the Emperor's right to mark the point. The two potentates divided their days into three parts. The mornings were devoted to political discussions, the afternoons to military reviews and hunting parties, and the evenings to receptions, balls and theatrical performances. The company of the Comédie Française was brought from Paris specially for the occasion. During a performance of Voltaire's *Oedipe* the Tsar suddenly stood up and pressed Napoleon's hand as the actor declaimed the line: "The friendship of a great man is a gift from the gods." Napoleon, for his part, captivated the aged Goethe by greeting him with the words: "You are a man." To the good German burghers of Erfurt the scene must have been dazzling—their city ablaze with uniforms, their narrow streets alive with soldiery, their opera house filled with the kings and captains of the two great empires, their tranquil countryside patterned by infantry and cavalry in ceremonial array. Ears deafened by saluting cannonry or charmed by the music accompanying the evening festivities, they stood in the streets to catch a glimpse of the two central figures, the Emperors of the West and of the East.

Yet beneath the surface dark currents were running strongly. The Tsar firmly resisted Napoleon's attempts to draw Russia into a menace against the Austrian Empire. Napoleon refused Alexander's request to withdraw French troops from Prussian fortresses or to approve Russian designs on Turkey. In the end all that Napoleon gained was recognition of Joseph as King of Spain and a joint note to George III summoning England to make peace. In public the two potentates were careful to give the appearance of being on the same terms of intimate friendship as at Tilsit. At dinner one evening Napoleon noticed that the Tsar had forgotten his sword. He immediately offered his own. When they were alone there were scenes. On one occasion Napoleon threw his hat on the ground in a fury and stamped on it. Alexander calmly remarked: "You are violent, I am obstinate. Let us talk reasonably, or I go."

The Tsar's suspicions of Napoleon were fostered by Talleyrand, Prince of Benevento, who told him bluntly: "It is for you to save Europe and you will only succeed in that by resisting Napoleon. The French are civilised, their sovereign is not. The sovereign of Russia is civilised, her people are not. Therefore the sovereign of Russia must be the ally of the French people." Méneval was aware that Talleyrand was betraying his sovereign and considered that Napoleon had committed not merely an imprudence but a fatal error in asking him to come to Erfurt. Talleyrand had been replaced as Minister for Foreign Affairs a year before (after the Tilsit meeting). He now held the highly distinguished offices of Grand Chamberlain and Vice-Grand Elector. His attendance at Erfurt was therefore not strictly necessary. But Talleyrand, as Méneval knew, had a fatal attraction for Napoleon. Every day he kept Talleyrand back after his morning levée at Erfurt and revealed to him his most secret thoughts. Every evening, when the formal festivities were ended, Talleyrand met the Tsar privately at the house of Princess Thurn and Taxis, and disclosed the Emperor's plans. The Tsar in turn told Talleyrand what had passed in his private talks with Napoleon.

This was treachery but it was what Duff Cooper in his biography of Talleyrand has called "treachery on a magnificent scale". Talleyrand had been profoundly shocked by the duplicity with which Napoleon had tricked the Spanish royal house in order to establish French domination over Spain. From that moment he saw in Napoleon a menace to Europe and worked for his overthrow. Talleyrand himself, a "European" in modern terms, was proud of the part he played at Erfurt. "It was the last service that I was able to render to Europe," he wrote in his memoirs, "so long as Napoleon continued to reign." As for Napoleon, success had gone to his head and it was inconceivable to him that an inferior being like Talleyrand, even though he knew him to be untrustworthy, could do him any real harm. He could, he thought, usefully be employed as a sharp-cutting instrument of the Master's grand designs.

When the time finally came for the two Emperors to take leave of each other, they stood in the road beside the carriages which were waiting to take the one to Paris, the other to St. Petersburg. Alexander, records Méneval, "embraced Napoleon with all the appearances of cordiality. They were to meet again, sword in hand." The meeting, in fact, did Napoleon more harm than good. It not only left the Russians deeply suspicious. It alarmed the rest of Europe and strengthened the British resolve to crush Napoleon.

Napoleon returned to Paris on October 19, 1808. If Pauline hoped that he would at last carry out his promise to concern himself with her affairs, she was disappointed, for he was hardly back before he was off on his travels again. This time his destination was the opposite end of his dominions. Matters were going badly in Spain. The French General Dupont had surrendered with 20,000 men at Baylen. A few weeks later the British landed a force near Lisbon under an unknown commander, Sir Arthur Wellesley. In late August, at Vimiero, Wellesley defeated Junot's force, and the French signed a convention obliging them to evacuate Portugal. King Joseph had been only five months on his uneasy throne in Madrid. Napoleon decided to assume personal command. After rushing reinforcements from Germany into Spain, he left St. Cloud on October 29. Establishing his headquarters first at Burgos for ten days, and then at Valladolid, he directed a series of masterly strokes against the disorganised Spanish forces and on December 4, 1808, entered Madrid in triumph. But his line of communication had been all but cut by another presumptuous British general moving against the French from Lisbon. Napoleon, after a brief stay in Madrid, turned to crush him. Sir John Moore, outnumbered, fought a gallant rearguard action and succeeded in embarking his small force at Corunna, but lost his own life. Napoleon, in after years, spoke generously of Moore as a brave soldier, an excellent officer and a man of talent.

Early in January news of such gravity reached Napoleon in Madrid that he decided on the instant to return to Paris. While he had been bringing the sullen Spaniards to heel and chasing the British out of Spain, the chancelleries of Europe and the

Parisian salons had not stood meekly by as mute spectators. Little was known about the Erfurt meeting. The worst was suspected, especially in Vienna. Was the Emperor Francis to be reduced to the position of a vassal of France, like the hapless King of Prussia; or even replaced on his throne by one of the Bonaparte brothers, like Charles IV of Spain? The Austrians started rearming. During these three months when the cat was away the mice had been playing with a vengeance. By the New Year of 1809 their game seemed really dangerous.

At home, too, a dangerous coalition was forming. One December evening in Paris in 1808 the Prince of Benevento had given one of his grand receptions. *Le Tout Paris* was there. When the name of Fouché, ex-Minister of the Interior, now head of the secret police, was announced, there was a buzz of excitement. Even Pauline, with her lack of interest in politics, could understand the significance of what followed.

Fouché and Talleyrand had been implacable enemies for so long as anyone remembered. When Talleyrand greeted his guest warmly and proceeded to promenade with him ostentatiously arm-in-arm through the crowded salons, the effect was electric. The lesson was not lost on the sophisticated company of politicians and gossips. This was an alliance between the only two really important figures who were known, each for his own reasons, to be critical of Napoleon's policies. Talleyrand the "European" foresaw Napoleon's extravagances after Austerlitz leading to the destruction of Europe as he knew it. Fouché, though even more of an opportunist than Talleyrand, was an ex-Terrorist and retained enough of his republican principles to be shocked by Napoleon's rapid evolution from the position of the saviour called in to stabilise the Republic to that of a self-willed illiberal dictator. When the news reached Napoleon, he lost no time. Méneval has described the furious stages of the Emperor's journey in mid-winter over the Spanish sierras. In a towering rage and using relays of horses, he rode "at such speed that his household could not follow him". On January 23, 1809, he was at the Tuileries—much to Pauline's relief.

Pauline was thankful when her brother returned to look after his interests. The moment he arrived in Paris Napoleon placed the French troops in the Rhineland on a war footing and put Berthier in command. He then summoned a restricted meeting of the privy council, at which Fouché as head of the secret police and Talleyrand as Vice-Elector were present. Fouché was not reproached. It is possible that Napoleon had already had a private talk alone with him and come to an understanding with this potentially dangerous adversary who knew so many secrets and controlled so many hidden forces. With Talleyrand there was no need for similar restraint. For half-an-hour without drawing breath Napoleon abused him up and down. Even Méneval thought the Emperor went rather far.

"You are a thief, a coward, a man without honour, you disbelieve in God, you have betrayed everyone, to you nothing is sacred, you would sell your own father. You suppose, without rhyme or reason, that my Spanish affairs are going wrong. You deserve to be smashed like a glass, but I despise you too profoundly to put myself to that trouble."

Talleyrand listened impassively till the tirade spent itself. "What a pity," he breathed in the ear of one of the embarrassed spectators, "that so great a man should be so ill-bred."

Napoleon did not judge Talleyrand by the standard of manners. As for Talleyrand's impassivity, he enjoyed recalling Murat's remark: "If somebody kicked him from behind while he was speaking to you, his face would show nothing."

Talleyrand was disgraced. Fouché ceased intriguing. When in his capital, Napoleon was entirely capable of controlling unruly elements; it was when he was away that conspiracy reared its head. As his ambitions expanded, as the subject states grew more restive, and the Austrians, still free, became more and more alarmed, he found himself constantly obliged to leave his capital and take the field. The trickery in Spain had alerted Europe. The Tsar's eyes had been opened at Erfurt to a realisation that the man whose charm had at first captivated him was a dangerous adventurer. During these dark January days in Paris at the opening of the year 1809 the tide was beginning to turn. Napoleon himself may already have been conscious, in personal terms, that he had set himself a pace which he could not keep up. He was forty—young still by the standards of a man leading a normal life. But he was conscious of the weight of those forty years. From Erfurt he had written to Joséphine: "I went to the ball at Weimar. The Emperor Alexander danced, but I didn't. Forty years of age are forty years!" Even after the battle of Austerlitz, when he was only thirty-six, he began to feel doubts whether he would have the force to continue at the same furious pace much longer.

Yet to outward appearances all was well. Napoleon's dramatic and sudden reappearances in the capital, always on the heels of a new series of military triumphs, never failed to have an invigorating effect on the Parisians. To so experienced a judge of social activity as Laure Junot, now Duchesse d'Abrantès since her husband had been honoured with a dukedom on his appointment to the Portuguese command in 1807, the Paris season of early 1809 seemed unusually brilliant. The German and Italian princes of the Empire flocked to Paris to pay their respects to the Emperor. Glittering receptions and balls, brilliant dinner parties were the order of the day. Gastronomy, under the inspired leadership of Cambacérès, Bonaparte's colleague as Second Consul and now Duke of Parma and Prince Arch-Chancellor of the Empire, reached unparalleled heights. In his beautifully furnished house in the rue Saint-Dominique the Arch-Chancellor gave suppers twice a week during the season. Many of the dishes, prepared by Carême, Cambacérès's cook, were delicacies sent by friends anxious to please the influential Arch-Chancellor: blackbirds obtained by the Duchesse d'Abrantès from her native Corsica; Mayence ham sent by Beugnot, administrator of the Grand Duchy of Berg; ortolans and thrushes from the prefect of the Basses-Pyrénées; and foie gras, pâtés and a variety of other delicacies from different parts of France. These "*réveillons gastronomiques*", at first confined to men, were opened to ladies exceptionally. Pauline attended the *réveillons* and many other parties, but hardly seemed to participate in them. She looked ill and languid and, while others danced, preferred to remain recumbent on her chaise-longue. To some it seemed that she loved to play the part of a languishing idol.

Yet Pauline, for all her enfeebled health, was happy. Napoleon at last, soon after his return from Spain, had personally gone into her financial affairs. Within ten days he sent his financial secretary round to explain the main outline of the settlement he proposed to make. She was to receive an annual income of 600,000 francs (about £168,000, 1964), separate from Camillo's income, and would in addition have the château of Neuilly at her disposal. Pauline was overjoyed. She had never expected anything so generous. The château had belonged to Murat and Caroline. On his assumption of the throne of Naples Murat was obliged to cede this property to the French state, in other words to Napoleon, who also profited by his brother-in-law's translation to make use of Murat's town house, the Palais de l'Elysée, three hundred yards down the Faubourg St. Honoré from Pauline's own home.

She went to see Napoleon and told him how grateful she was. Her gratitude was not only for the generosity of the financial settlement and the tenure of Neuilly. She was even more pleased by the prospect of being financially independent of Camillo. She was truly grateful. He was charming and affectionate. She wrote warmly to Murat about Napoleon's kindness. She felt well, she was putting on weight. "The Emperor," she added, "has put on a lot of weight."

The building Pauline was given had been started in 1751 by the Comte d'Argenson, *Intendant de la Généralité de Paris* (i.e. Prefect of the Seine), in the "Roman style". After d'Argenson's disgrace owing to the intervention of Madame de Pompadour, whose displeasure he had incurred, the château passed through various hands and was rented by Talleyrand in 1800. In 1804 it was bought by Murat, then Governor of Paris. He added the two wings to the central *corps de logis*, and, with the help of Caroline, redecorated and furnished the château in the new Empire style.

A few weeks later, on February 1, 1809, Napoleon sent Pauline a statement in great detail which gave effect to the new financial arrangements. It in fact increased her income and secured her tenure of the château of Neuilly by incorporating it in her Duchy of Guastalla. With an income of over a million francs a year of her own, Pauline was now a very rich woman. In the first days of spring she moved into the château of Neuilly and was delighted with what she found. Murat had taken very little with him to Naples. Napoleon had merely removed some marble statues which he sent to Compiègne, and some Etruscan vases which he sent to Malmaison. Pauline was glad to be rid of any statuesque objects that might recall the interior of the Palazzo Borghese in Rome where she had been so miserable. She surveyed with joy the severe but ornate decorations and furnishings in the most sumptuous Empire style of which she had become so fond that it now seemed her natural setting, and turned happily to the work of rearranging the house to her taste and deciding which pieces of furniture to transport to the hôtel in the Faubourg St. Honoré, which up to now she had never been able to furnish completely.

The château was set near the Seine in a large park occupying most of the modern suburb of Neuilly. Pauline had only to turn to the left along the rue du Faubourg St. Honoré and half-an-hour's drive down the gently curving Faubourg brought her to the post-gates of her newly acquired property. A long avenue led to the low entrance façade of the château, flanked on either side by the wings built by Murat and Caroline. On the further side of the central façade lawns sloped gently down to the Seine. It was a beautiful house, and a large one. Fortunately she now had an ample income to keep it up and at the same time maintain her town house, as well as undertake journeys in search of better health.

The château continued to be linked with the rulers of France long after it was confiscated from Pauline on Napoleon's downfall. The Duc d'Orléans (the future King Louis Philippe) acquired it by exchange from Louis XVIII after the Restoration, and enlarged it. It was his favourite residence after he became king in 1830. During the revolution of 1848 which cost him his throne, most of the château was burnt, only the right-hand wing, the "Pavillon de Madame Adélaïde", surviving. In 1907 the Religieuses de Saint-Thomas de Villeneuve acquired this pavilion. It is still in an excellent state of preservation, and though hemmed in by modern buildings (and occupying only two and a half acres of the vast park of Pauline's day), gives a clear impression of what this elegant and luxurious residence must have looked like in the early nineteenth century when Pauline reigned there.

For all her wildness and extravagance Pauline kept a close and businesslike eye on her affairs. The splendid modern furniture and ornaments with which Murat and Caroline had equipped Neuilly were made to serve the Paris house as well until she had enough money to furnish it to her taste. Pieces were regularly carried back and forth between the two great houses. Finally Pauline decided it would be more economical not to incur the expense of transport. "I desire," she wrote, "that everything at Neuilly, like dressing-tables, vases, clocks, couches, etc., should stay at Neuilly and not be carried backwards and forwards as has been done up to now." When she decided to transform the old eighteenth-century chapel on the first floor of the Hôtel de Charost into a billiard room (a room now used as a small dining-room in the Embassy), she gave precise instructions about the alterations. There was to be no undue expense. A good billiard table and cues were authorised. But there was no need to buy new chairs. Eight could be spared from the ante-room on the ground floor. This careful attention to the detail of organisation and finance was, like everything else with Pauline, capricious. It waxed and waned according to the state of her health and her emotions.

Napoleon was never far from her thoughts nowadays. As a child she had admired her dazzling, heroic elder brother. As he climbed to power and as she grew to early womanhood she had

sometimes come near to hating him. He had prevented her
marrying the man she loved, foisted on her when a young widow
a husband she had cause to detest, and had forced her to follow
both husbands to parts of the world where she never wanted to
go. But the harsh memories of San Domingo and the miseries
of Turin were becoming softened by time. Once she had quivered
with indignation under the reproofs and threats, the staccato
military commands she used to receive from her brother. She had
bitterly resented his lack of sympathy when she was ill and
miserable in Piedmont and he had scarcely bothered to answer
her appeals. But in the end he had relented and understood. All
her native clannishness, her natural loyalty, welled up from its
hidden springs in her complex being. He was not only her
brother; he was the Emperor. She longed to gain his confidence, to help him with understanding and affection.

She was at Neuilly when in April 1809 Napoleon left to take
the field against the Austrians who had crossed the Bavarian
frontier on the 1st. She knew the frenzied efforts he had been
making since the New Year to assemble adequate forces to fight
a war that was none of his choosing and from which he could
gain little. She heard with relief that Vienna had been occupied
without difficulty in May. Then the news reached Paris that the
Archduke Charles had defeated him at Essling. It was Napoleon's
first reverse. She had thought him invincible. It was not till
she heard of the decisive though murderous victory of Wagram
on July 6, and the armistice that followed, that Pauline, her mind
at rest, felt able to make plans to join her mother and sister-in-
law for the summer.

Even her restored health and the novelty of Neuilly could not
break the habit of years. Though not yet thirty, Pauline was a
confirmed valetudinarian. She could never stay long away from
a watering-place. Her youngest brother Jérôme, who had
married Princess Catherine of Württemberg after giving up the
American Miss Patterson at Napoleon's behest, was King of
Westphalia. From him Pauline learnt that there was an excellent
cure at Aachen. Aachen was a novelty; it was also fashionable.

So to Aachen Pauline went at the end of July, 1809. Madame Mère and the Queen of Westphalia had already been there for about a fortnight. The three Imperial ladies all travelled incognito under assumed names. "Madame de Ramolino," "Gräfin von Mansfeldt," and Pauline herself as "Comtesse de Bassano" were soon joined by King Louis of Holland. There were relatively few attendants. It was a family party. Napoleon's agent in the Grand Duchy of Berg, Beugnot, who saw her that summer at Aachen, was struck by her beauty, "the typical French beauty, that is to say beauty refined and enlivened by gaiety". Certainly Pauline was in high spirits and enjoyed herself madly. The family and Dr. Peyre looked on approvingly. Pauline seemed a normal young woman again.

15. Joséphine
1809

NAPOLEON STAYED IN VIENNA FOR THREE MONTHS WHILE the terms of peace were being painfully hammered out by Champagny and Metternich, the French and Austrian plenipotentiaries. The Austrians were forced to reaffirm the arrangements affecting Italy which had been agreed at Pressburg in 1805 and to make further sacrifices of territory to the Napoleonic Empire, including Istria and Illyria, the last remaining sea-board of the Austrian Empire, which thus became a land-locked power. The Treaty was signed on October 14, 1809, and Napoleon left Vienna the next day. Leaving nothing to chance, he remained in Germany until the Treaty was ratified, and returned to Fontainebleau, unannounced, at 9 a.m. on October 29. Pauline immediately left Aachen and hurried back to Paris.

At the earliest opportunity she went to Fontainebleau to see her brother. The first thing he told her was that he had decided to divorce Joséphine. For the next few weeks little else was talked of at the court. Pauline was overjoyed to hear that at last Napoleon had made his mind up to take this step. She had disliked Joséphine even before they met face to face and had for long considered her unworthy of her great brother. There was another reason for rejoicing. With her brothers and sisters abroad in their kingdoms and principalities, Pauline would now be the principal lady of the Imperial family in Paris. She could see herself at the Tuileries or the Elysée, at St. Cloud or Fontainebleau, at the Emperor's left hand, receiving Paris society and the princes and princesses of the Empire. When she was tired of pomp and ceremony, would anyone refuse to come to Neuilly, to the joyous small parties of the principal lady in the land?

She was aghast when she heard of Napoleon's intention to marry the Austrian Archduchess, Marie Louise. To get rid of Joséphine was one thing; to replace her by the daughter of one of the greatest Houses of Europe was quite another—a young woman who by her position as Empress of the French and as daughter of a long line of monarchs would outshine and put her sister-in-law utterly in the shade. Pauline did not like the prospect at all. But, being entirely without political ambition and no longer caring intensely about her own position, she soon forgot her disappointment and certainly did not show it to Napoleon. She became her brother's sympathetic confidante during these weeks of indecision.

Napoleon was torn between conflicting emotions and conflicting interests. He knew that Joséphine had betrayed him many times in the past. Everyone told him she was no longer capable of bearing children, though he had a nagging suspicion that he was the partner who was at fault in progenitiveness, since Joséphine had had two children by Beauharnais. She was the only woman, in spite of the difference in their ages, in whose arms he was certain of finding happiness. Still, he must have a child—a son. It was the succession, not the divorce, that mattered most. Then there was his position as Emperor of the French. He could not be for ever the Corsican *arriviste*, he must ally himself with the traditional monarchies. The last Austrian campaign had been a terrible struggle. He felt his forty-two years. The Austrians were sullen, longing for revenge. The Erfurt meeting had been a failure; the Russians were suspicious. The damned English were causing trouble in Spain. Joseph was quaking on his shaky throne in Madrid and the British general, Wellesley, was beating his best Marshals. He felt the world crowding in on him—Austria and Russia at one end of Europe, Spain at the other.

For the past decade Napoleon had been imperious, making his ascent to the summit of power. His brothers and sisters were treated as pawns in the Imperial game. Lucien alone had rebelled and withdrawn as a player. As for Pauline, loyalty and indolence prevented her from going to such extremes, although she had deeply resented his lack of consideration, his cold cruelty to her on occasion. But that was already half forgiven. She was eager to play her part. It was a joy to find that, beset with increasing anxieties, he was less inaccessible, more human. She began to rediscover the elder brother she had idolised. Her natural affection was revived and her admiration for the head of the clan engaged. Brother and sister were suddenly on terms of equality and affection.

Pauline understood the complicated relationship which had for so many years stood the test of continuous differences between Napoleon and Joséphine. He had often deceived her. There had been many women in his life. But not even the charming Madame de Vaudey, the love of his days as First Consul, or the twenty-year-old Madame Duchâtel about whom he had had such terrible scenes with Joséphine soon after he became Emperor, had been able to hold him. Napoleon, she knew, was strangely awkward with all women except Joséphine. But there was a Polish countess for whom he was reported to have a real passion. He had met Marie Walewska in Warsaw during the winter of 1806-7. She fell deeply in love with him, but would not have betrayed her elderly husband had she not been persuaded that she must yield for the sake of Poland.

Napoleon courted Marie by letter as well as word of mouth, while continuing to write affectionately an almost daily letter to Joséphine. On New Year's Eve 1806 he wrote to Joséphine, waiting in Mainz for permission to come on to Warsaw: "I have had a good laugh over your last letters. You idealise the fair ones of Great Poland in a way they do not deserve."

On New Year's Day he met Marie Walewska.

"Warsaw, January 2, 1807. To Countess Walewska.
"I saw only you, I admired you. I desire only you. A quick answer will calm the impatient ardour of   N."

The next day he wrote to Joséphine: "I am inclined to think

144

The Salon Blanc et Or in the British Embassy, used by Pauline as her private drawing-room. In the corner is a model of Canova's statue of Pauline; above it hangs the sculptor's portrait by Sir George Hayter, and in the mirror can be seen the portrait of Pauline as a girl

Photo Z. Mihanoff, Paris

Pauline's state bed, surmounted by the Napoleonic eagle, its sphinxes and caryatids commemorating Napoleon's Egyptian campaign, and Napoleon's looking-glass—both in the British Embassy in Paris

Photo R. Bonnefoy, Paris

Canova's statue of Pauline Bonaparte (1804) in the Palazzo Borghese, Rome

Photo Anderson

you had better go back to Paris. I am well. The weather is wretched. I love you from my heart."

Marie was still resisting nine days later, when Napoleon wrote: "Oh come! come! All your wishes shall be complied with. Your country will become more dear to me if you take compassion on my poor heart.   *N.*"

The insidious shaft went home. How could a patriotic Pole, who in any case was in love with this extraordinary man, resist the master of Europe? Marie yielded.

"Marie, my sweet Marie," he wrote on the 15th; "you will come again, will you not? You promised that you would. If not, the eagle will wing his way to you!"

The next day he wrote to Joséphine: "I shall see you soon. Never doubt my feelings . . . I am humiliated to think my wife can distrust my destinies." On the 18th he was urging her to "show more character" and to return to Paris. "An Empress ought to have fortitude."

By this time Joséphine, still waiting at Mainz, had found out about Marie. Her agitation was indescribable. She implored permission to join him in Warsaw. Napoleon continued to cajole and reason with her, to no avail. Finally he wrote sternly:

"It is out of the question that I should allow women to undertake such a journey; bad roads, unsafe, and quagmires. Go back to Paris. Be gay and happy . . . Goodbye, dear friend; pray believe that I regret not being able to send for you. Say to yourself: Here is proof how precious I am to him."

From the tone of this letter Joséphine understood that the battle was lost. She set off miserably on the road back to Paris, from where she continued to write reproachfully. In the spring of 1807 Napoleon openly took Marie off to live with him at his headquarters at the Castle of Finckenstein. All was reported to Joséphine.

"I love only my little Joséphine," he wrote on May 10; "sweet, sulky, capricious. She is always lovable except when she is jealous, and then she becomes a little devil."

This, Pauline knew, exactly expressed Napoleon's feelings

towards Joséphine. So long as she turned a blind eye to his escapades, he still loved the "sweet, sulky, capricious" woman, now nearly fifty, to whom he had been married for thirteen tempestuous years. Pauline knew the inexplicable hold that Joséphine had over her brother and was desperately anxious to see it broken for good. She therefore welcomed the prospect of a divorce. But she very much disliked the idea of the young Austrian Archduchess sitting on the Imperial throne. It would be much more satisfactory if Napoleon divorced Joséphine and lived happily with his Polish countess. But here another complex in Napoleon's character had to be reckoned with. By the time he met her, Marie had already had a son by the seventy-year-old Count Walewski. Yet, after two years together, she had shown no signs of making Napoleon a father. A few years earlier his fears about his capacity for fatherhood had been temporarily set at rest. Caroline, Princess Murat, well aware of her brother's secret fear and desiring to prove that Joséphine was the incapable partner, had introduced him to an eighteen-year-old girl, Eléonore de La Plaigne, whom she had taken into her household at Neuilly. To his indescribable joy and relief, Eléonore within the year bore him a son. He lost interest in Eléonore herself as soon as he set eyes on Marie Walewska. But suddenly the old fear revived under a new suspicion. The girl had been living under Murat's roof when Caroline had forced her on his attention. He confronted Eléonore with his suspicions. She confessed that Murat had been her lover at the same time. Napoleon realised with horror that there could be no certainty of the paternity of the child, though he treated Eléonore's son generously. How well Pauline understood his feelings and his longing for fatherhood. The image of her little Dermid rose vividly to her mind.

As she saw deeper and deeper into her brother's complex anxieties, Pauline understood that personal pride and reasons of state all tended in the same direction. He felt an absolute need to marry a young girl who would give him an heir and guarantee the succession, and the bride must belong to a great royal house so that the dynasty could be firmly allied to the reigning houses of Europe. He had been toying with the idea for some time. At Erfurt in September 1808 he had instructed Talleyrand to sound out the Tsar about the possibility of one of his sisters marrying the Emperor of the French. But nothing had come of this move, which Talleyrand did not press very hard. Both Talleyrand and Metternich, the Austrian Ambassador in Paris, favoured an alliance with the house of Austria.

It was not what Pauline wanted. If he could not be content with Marie Walewska, why could he not marry his niece, Lolotte, Lucien's daughter? This did not suit Napoleon. It must be a dynastic alliance. Pauline saw that his mind was made up. But at least the main point was gained—the dismissal of Joséphine. Or was it? Napoleon arrived from Austria at Fontainebleau on October 29, 1809. Nearly three weeks later he had still not brought himself to break the news to her. Pauline was at his side during most of this period of agonising uncertainty. Her sympathy was genuine, she really wished to be a support to her brother at this climacteric of his personal and official career. Pauline was not a natural intriguer, like most of her sisters and brothers. She would never have played a scurvy trick such as Caroline's when she used Eléonore de La Plaigne to further the Family's plan to have Joséphine divorced. True, Pauline was lacking in a sense of morality, and when Napoleon's roving eye was caught by the plump prettiness of Madame de Mathis, one of her Italian ladies-in-waiting at Turin whom she had brought back with her to France, Pauline, as has already been recorded, went to unusual lengths to persuade the reluctant beauty to surrender. The news was all round Fontainebleau that month of November.

Napoleon had returned to Fontainebleau resolved to inform Joséphine firmly of his intentions. Instead, there had been a terrible scene, ending, as these scenes always had over the years, with Joséphine in tears and Napoleon shaken, practically a physical wreck. "This man," records Méneval, "whom many people have long considered as pitiless, dreaded the sight of tears and affliction, against which as a matter of fact he was always defenceless. I have often seen him, after a scene with Joséphine, so troubled that he would remain in his workroom given up to silent emotion and unable to resume his work." This time it was Joséphine who locked herself behind doors, through which her sobs were audible. Napoleon consoled himself with Madame de Mathis. For more than two weeks nothing was said. Divorce, the fatal word, was still not spoken. On November 16, Napoleon abruptly moved the court to Paris, as if, somehow, it would be easier to be stern at the Tuileries than at Fontainebleau. But another fortnight passed and still he could not bring himself to the striking point.

On November 30 they were dining alone in Napoleon's private apartments at the Tuileries. "After," as Méneval says, "the most silent and sorrowful of meals," he took the plunge and announced his irrevocable decision. Joséphine uttered a shriek of despair, and fainted. Napoleon's agitation was extreme. He called the waiting attendant and asked him to carry the Empress down the private stairs that communicated with her apartments. When they reached the head of the stairs, Napoleon carrying a candlestick to light the way, the man said that they were too narrow for him to carry the prostrate woman down without falling. Another attendant was summoned, and between them, with Napoleon holding her legs, they managed to carry Joséphine to her room. The next day Napoleon recorded: "Joséphine sent me word that she consented." On December 15 Napoleon requested the Privy Council to meet and move the Senate to adopt a Senatus Consultum decreeing that "the marriage contracted between the Emperor Napoleon and the Empress Joséphine is dissolved".

Pauline was present, with Madame Mère and other members of the family, at the ceremonial final meeting between the Emperor and the discarded Empress. Joséphine was calm and resigned, Napoleon in tears; the Bonaparte family, in their hour of triumph, were also in tears. Even Pauline could not find it in her heart to blame her brother for his generous treatment of Joséphine, who retained her Imperial titles and received an Imperial allowance. Nor was she disturbed to hear that Napoleon and Joséphine continued to see each other and exchange affectionate letters. The die, she knew, was irrevocably cast. That was enough. And she herself, from all this turmoil and anguish, had emerged as the sister who had helped and sustained Napoleon, to whom she thought she could henceforward confidently look for support.

16. La Vie Joyeuse: Canouville

1810-11

THE EPISODE OF THE DIVORCE MADE A DIFFERENCE TO THE relationship between Pauline and Napoleon. He let her do much more as she pleased. The days were over when he insisted on her keeping up the appearances of a normal conjugal life with Borghese and holding court with him as part of the visible panoply of the Napoleonic Empire. He no longer upbraided her continuously for her follies and was more inclined to turn a blind eye to her indiscretions, so long as they did not touch the Emperor's dignity or affect Imperial interests. Those three weeks at Fontainebleau, when Pauline had been the only human being to whom he could open his heart and who understood that the *raison d'état* must prevail over personal inclination, had been a turning-point for both of them. For Pauline, as well as Napoleon. She understood that this was no ordinary brother. Not only was he the fount of munificence (and she was genuinely grateful for his generosity); he was the Emperor. So Pauline determined to do what she could to add lustre to the Imperial court and to be more discreet in her private life. In the event, neither brother nor sister was very successful in this new approach to mutual tolerance.

For the moment Pauline turned happily to her new house at Neuilly as an ideal setting for her new resolutions. Against this magnificent background she could receive *tout Paris* in a manner worthy of the Emperor's sister. Away from the centre of Paris, but not so far away as to be inaccessible, she could see her friends quietly without the gossips automatically knowing whom she saw.

She built grottoes and little pavilions in the gardens. She made a suite of enchanting private apartments in the château—

a salon with walls lined in blue silk, another in green silk and another in silk of a chocolate colour. Her bedroom was blue, her dressing-room orange, and the gallery which looked over the park down to the Seine was decorated in crimson. The salons in the house in the Faubourg St. Honoré were similarly hung in silk of varied colours. But in both houses there was the same prevailing severity in the Empire chairs, settees, mirrors and fire-places. Pauline found her natural setting in this combination of gaiety and style.

All these transformations cost money. Early in the New Year of 1810 Napoleon had made still more generous arrange-ments to secure his sister's future. Besides paying off her debts, he made her advances of income well beyond that of the settle-ment of the previous year, crowning all with the gift of a splendid parure of turquoises. Knowing how extravagant she was, he provided her, in his own interests as well as hers, with an *intendant général*, an administrator, in whom he had confidence. This man, J. P. L. Michelot, proved himself a pearl beyond price. Pauline herself quickly came to understand his worth. Together they managed her affairs so satisfactorily that henceforward she never had to concern herself seriously with money matters, and when the Empire finally collapsed it was Michelot who arranged the sale of the Hôtel de Charost and thereby helped to secure her financial position in exile.

Her newly acquired sense of money as well as her inclination led Pauline to be strictly businesslike in her dealings with Camillo Borghese. She insisted that, in accordance with the separation of their incomes laid down in Napoleon's arrangements, he should pay for the cost of his meals and those of his attendants when he came to stay in the Hôtel de Charost or the Château de Neuilly. Camillo did not relish being treated as a lodger in his wife's house, and still less being told not to make so much noise on the first floor of the Hôtel de Charost, which Pauline felt obliged to put at his disposal during his infrequent and unwelcome visits. Camillo did not care much for Paris anyway, and his visits became rarer and rarer.

On April 2, 1810, the marriage of Napoleon and Marie Louise was celebrated at the Louvre. Pauline had at first refused to hold the Archduchess's train and, when Napoleon insisted, had done so with ill grace, though it is not recorded that she deliberately tugged on the train as she had done at Joséphine's coronation. Train-bearing certainly was not Pauline's *forte*. Perhaps from contrition at her ungracious behaviour, perhaps because she owed some return for her brother's generosity, Pauline decided to give a fête at Neuilly in honour of the Emperor and the new Empress. It was a splendid affair, of which every detail was arranged by Pauline herself with the help of Michelot. It was still daylight when Napoleon and Marie Louise arrived punctually at nine o'clock on that midsummer evening. Pauline received them in one of Leroy's latest creations, a short-waisted classical robe *à l'Etrusque*. The proceedings opened with a musical play, *La Danse Interrompue*. The play finished, the Emperor and Empress proceeded into the park, illuminated with fairy lights. Suddenly living statues leapt down from their pedestals and conducted the royal pair to a Temple of Hymen. From there they were led through this fairyland to a miniature reproduction of the Palace of Schoenbrunn, Marie Louise's home outside Vienna. Then there were fireworks, and at midnight the ball was opened. All this was noted and described by several of the guests who wrote memoirs of the occasion. Napoleon enjoyed the evening so much that he asked Pauline to repeat the performance the following week—to Pauline's dismay, because of the expense.

For ten years Pauline had not been in such high spirits. The reconciliation with Napoleon, the sudden wealth and the possession of a splendid country house, the feeling that she was free of Camillo, her improved health—all contributed to an outburst of energy such as she had not been capable of for a decade. She gave a ball every Thursday and a concert every Saturday. People flocked to her parties, and there were those she asked to stay behind after the party was over. This was certainly a period when, once again, she felt a compelling need for masculine company. Metternich, the Austrian Ambassador, was a frequent visitor. There was a string of young foreigners, members of the suites of the monarchs who had come to Paris for the royal wedding. There was a Russian officer, Tchernichev; a Polish officer, Poniatowski; a German officer, Friedrich. Pauline had always liked military men and at this time at any rate, showed a marked inclination towards foreigners. The Parisians chattered and gossiped, and so did the favoured foreigners. Pauline was in-different to chatter and gossip and would not have cared if she had known that several of these gentlemen were carefully record-ing their experiences. The youngest of them all, Conrad Fried-rich, has left a highly imaginative account of an encounter with Pauline and her ladies in one of the artificial grottoes in the park at Neuilly which reads like a scene out of the *Nibelungenlied*.

Though this episode has generally been taken as an example of Pauline's depravity, it is difficult to resist the impression, on reading Friedrich's meticulous and disapproving chronicle, that Pauline was having a joke of her own special kind at the expense of the impressionable though doubtless handsome young Teuton. The secret assignation in a remote part of the park, the long wait under a colonnade before a romantic grotto, the smiling attendant in flowing robes who at last beckoned him into a mysterious interior, the pool in which they bathed (also in flowing robes) and the operatic style of feast which followed— all suggests a display of theatre which Pauline and her ladies no doubt greatly enjoyed at the expense of a serious-minded young foreigner.

For Metternich, Pauline was "as pretty as it is possible to be. She was in love with herself, and her only occupation was pleasure." This, no doubt, was a true impression, recorded by an experienced observer, of what Pauline was like in this joyous year 1810.

It is doubtful whether Pauline's escapades with these youthful foreigners were very serious affairs. Certainly her affections were in no case deeply engaged. But later in the summer she met a

Frenchman, Jules de Canouville, and this time it was a *coup de foudre*.

Jules de Canouville, a Hussar officer on Berthier's staff, was a typical product of the age of the Napoleonic wars. Madame de Rémusat lamented that the young officers in the Emperor's entourage were men in a hurry, with no time for the patient processes of true love, eager only for swift victory. Such a man was Canouville. His appeal to the thirty-year-old Pauline was instantaneous; her surrender was immediate; and since there were for the moment no real wars to be fought, the conquest was durable. They met during the summer of 1810 and he occupied the centre of Pauline's thoughts until his death more than two years later. Unfortunately for Pauline, Canouville was not a docile or a discreet lover. So far, however, the liaison had not reached Napoleon's ears, or, if he had heard of it, he was indulgent, remembering how Pauline had helped him during the agonising period of indecision leading up to the Divorce. She was able to arrange for Canouville to be at Fontainebleau, in attendance on Berthier, when she went to spend the autumn there with the court. She was amiability itself to Marie Louise and supported without complaint the interminable routine of dinners, excursions and concerts. Anything was tolerable when Canouville was waiting for her at the end of each day. With incredible imprudence she arranged for her favourite's services to be suitably rewarded: in October he was created a baron of the Empire. The new baron for his part was not the man to conceal a conquest of which he was in fact extremely proud. The inevitable happened. Early in November the Emperor was informed and immediately instructed Berthier to find a pretext to send Canouville to the Portuguese front. Canouville galloped off like a madman but was soon back in France; Berthier nevertheless thought it prudent to send him off once more to the Iberian peninsula. He was not to see Pauline again for twelve months.

Fontainebleau, where she had been so happy the previous autumn, and this year till the blow fell, was now intolerable to

Pauline. She left without taking leave of the Emperor and hurried to the Hôtel de Charost, where the staff were not expecting her. She was furious with Napoleon, after all she felt she had done to help him. She was also indignant for another reason —his treatment of Louis. Throughout his career Napoleon was embroiled with his family, expecting them to act their parts in the great game of Empire, raging against them when they behaved as their very individualistic selves. Lucien he had long dismissed as impossible. He had grave doubts about Joseph, who was not proving resolute enough in Spain. Even young Jérôme, who had always done what he was told, was proving unsatisfactory in his comfortable little kingdom of Westphalia. Napoleon had felt obliged to read him a stern lesson, reminding him that he was a king and a brother of the Emperor. "You have much ambition," he wrote, "some intelligence, a few good qualities, but spoilt by silliness and great presumption, and you have no real knowledge." Caroline and Elisa were no better, with their interminable arguing and insatiable lust for money and position. Of Caroline he wrote in exasperation: "With her it's always a pitched battle. To bring a chit of a woman of my own family to reason, I must needs deliver harangues as long as if she were the Senate and the Council of State together." Even his mother, whom he loved, was ridiculous as the mother of the Emperor—"She was too parsimonious."

And now Louis. At this moment when the most rigorous application of the Continental System was required, when England could not be brought to heel unless the commercial war was pursued with the utmost vigour, the King of Holland blatantly allowed British goods to flow into the Low Countries. Remonstrances, threats against Dutch trade, were of no avail. The unbelievable truth was borne in upon Napoleon: Louis was not prepared to regard himself as a lieutenant of the Emperor; he thought himself an independent monarch ruling by divine right! Napoleon was outraged. It was all so clear to him. Holland, Naples, Westphalia, Spain, for convenience and appearance' sake were independent kingdoms; but surely the brothers and sister he had placed on these splendid thrones should understand that in reality these units were part of an Empire, a family concern run by the head of the Family? Very well, if Louis would not play the family game, he must take the consequences. To maintain the appearance of independence, Holland had an ambassador in France and France an ambassador in Holland. "I shall not maintain an ambassador in Holland any longer," Napoleon wrote furiously to his brother on May 23, 1810; "but leave only a chargé d'affaires." The threat left Louis unmoved. Finally Napoleon resorted to the ultimate sanction. A strong French force moved on Amsterdam. On July 1 Louis abdicated and fled to Bohemia, travelling under the name of Comte de St. Leu, a title taken from the name of a property of his near Paris. A week later Holland was annexed to the French Empire. Louis went to live in Graz.

The whole of the Bonaparte family took the part of Louis, and Pauline was openly critical of Napoleon. She expressed herself forcibly in letters which Louis, from distant Styria, answered in similar vein. Napoleon's secret police were instructed to intercept all letters passing between members of the family and Louis. At least one from Pauline escaped the net. Napoleon wrote angrily to the director-general of posts: "I am annoyed you let through Princess Pauline's letter to the Comte de St. Leu."

The consequences were unfortunate for Pauline. Napoleon could be mean, and he requited her espousal of Louis's cause by breaking up her affair with Canouville. From now onwards she became a subject of interest to the secret police.

Napoleon's irritation with his family was understandable. As autumn gave way to winter his preoccupations increased, at home and abroad, and, for the first time for years he found it desirable to curb his restless lust for travel from one end of Europe to the other. He stayed in Paris in order to control events from the centre. At home the clericals were incensed by the imprisonment of the Pope, the intrigues of the Royalists were mounting. Abroad, the situation in Spain was a constant anxiety, with the English under Wellington making progress, and Joseph incapable of controlling the rivalries of the French marshals or assuaging the outraged national sentiment of the Spaniards. The Continental blockade against England was not effective. The Russian attitude was disturbing. At the end of February 1811 Napoleon was constrained to warn the Tsar that an understanding between Russia and England would be equivalent to the beginning of war "between our two Empires". At the same time he still had his eye on the Orient. Agents were sent to inspect the defences of Syria and Egypt and stores were assembled at Toulon for a descent on Egypt.

While the war clouds were gathering, the sky in Paris had never been more brilliant than in that winter of 1810-11. On February 26, 1811, there was a masked ball at the Tuileries which Pauline, who had offered to devise a quadrille, was determined to make the most dazzling ever known. The quadrille, it seems, was not a success. After the ball the young Empress, far advanced in pregnancy, was taken ill, and messages were hastily sent to members of the family abroad to come at once to Paris. To Pauline's disgust Camillo took the opportunity to leave Turin and install himself in the Hôtel de Charost. On March 19 the family were summoned to the Tuileries, with the members of the Senate and the Municipality. They waited all night, and were dismissed by Napoleon in the early morning, as the birth was after all not expected to be imminent. Thankfully Pauline returned to the Hôtel de Charost and her *lit de poupée*. Hardly had she closed her eyes than she heard the sound of cannon. In Napoleon's own words: "At eight Dubois [the doctor] ran in. He was pale as death and very agitated. I shouted to him, 'Well, is she dead? If she is dead, we will have a funeral!' . . . Dubois answered no, but that the child presented itself sideways . . . I ran down quickly to the Empress's apartments. She was screaming horribly . . . The King of Rome was at least a minute before he uttered a sound. As I came in he was lying on the carpet as though dead . . . The Empress had thought it was all over with her; she was convinced that she would be sacrificed for the child; and yet I had said that the opposite should be done."

Pauline and Camillo hastily dressed for the second time and hurried back to the Tuileries. They arrived soon after 9 a.m. and put their signatures to the birth certificate. Early in June they again went to the Tuileries together and drove in procession to Notre Dame for the ceremonial christening of the heir to the French Empire. Pauline, all rancour momentarily forgotten, understood what this event meant to her brother: the certain satisfaction, at last, of his longing for paternity, the vision of the perpetuation of the dynasty of the new Charlemagne. Nothing is more human about Napoleon than his affection for this child, and his anxiety about his fate during the years of misery at St. Helena. The boy's portrait, with those of Marie Louise and Joséphine, were on the mantelpiece at Longwood before his dying eyes. He was spared the knowledge of l'Aiglon's miserable end in confinement at Vienna.

Throughout that summer of 1811 the birth of Napoleon's heir and the splendour of the Empire were celebrated by balls, fêtes and public displays of the most varied and ingenious kind. In the park of St. Cloud the climax of a *fête champêtre* was an ascent in a balloon by Madame Blanchard, a famous lady aeronaut of the day, who remained floating for some time on a level with the tops of the trees. Pauline joined in the festivities enthusiastically and gave two balls in June at Neuilly. Her duty done, she left in early July for Aachen.

She was ill again, and brooded about Canouville. The arrival of Madame Mère cheered her up, as it always did. There was genuine affection between mother and daughter, and the Signora undoubtedly had a calming influence on Pauline. With improving health, however, the familiar cycle started again. She began to feel the need of excitement, the excitement she liked best. Aachen was empty that season, or Pauline would not have spent as much time as she did in the company of so disreputable a character as the Comte de Montrond, a notorious man-about-town who was not above acting as an informer for Talleyrand.

A dissipated quinquagenarian was an unusual choice of companion for Pauline, who preferred youth and vigour, but he had the reputation of an amusing talker, and Pauline was in need of distraction. Montrond and his flow of malicious society gossip, and the more congenial personality of a Russian colonel, Platon Ivanovitch Kabloukoff, served to keep her amused. When she left for Spa in early September both men attached themselves to her suite.

All this was noted by the secret police, who had been carefully surveying Pauline since Napoleon had heard of her indiscreet correspondence with Louis. They had nothing really damaging or scandalous to report, but Napoleon was once more displeased with his sister. On September 24 she stayed a few days in Brussels on her way back to Paris. Marie Louise was in the royal palace at Laeken, waiting to join Napoleon who was expected at Antwerp at the end of the month. It was certainly Pauline's duty to wait on the Empress, who, for her part, sent polite enquiries about her sister-in-law's health. Pauline was ill, but not so ill as to be incapable of undertaking the short drive to Laeken. Yet she could not bring herself to make the effort. Marie Louise was upset and complained to Napoleon when they met at Antwerp on the 30th. A few days later Napoleon ordered Montrond's arrest.

Things were again going badly between Pauline and Napoleon. Worse was to come. When she returned to Paris she was overjoyed to hear that Canouville was back. They started seeing each other again. But even the comparative secrecy of their meetings at Neuilly was not proof against the Imperial Secret Service. On November 24 Napoleon ordered Berthier to pack Canouville off to Danzig the very same day.

IV

Pale Misfeature

17. "Oh, Napoleon, what have you done?"
1811-14

THE FATEFUL YEAR 1812 OPENED WITH THE CUSTOMARY round of festivities. There were two state balls at the Tuileries. Pauline gave a ball at the Hôtel de Charost. The ambassadors and the Parisian hostesses held receptions. In the nightly round of social activities Pauline found the stimulus which her frivolous nature required. Tinsel and chandeliers, play-acting and quadrilles, were her natural milieu. The winter season in Imperial Paris suited her to perfection. It was the substitute for deeper emotions, the cure for morbid distempers. She enjoyed the admiration which her febrile beauty universally excited. She took infinite pains in devising the elaborate symbolical quadrilles which had become fashionable under the Empire. Napoleon was far from complimentary about the quadrille in which Pauline appeared as Italy and Caroline as France and the two sisters joined hands and danced happily together. They had thought it such a brilliant idea to depict the unity of France and Italy. They were sure it would appeal to Napoleon. But the Emperor thought the historical symbolism out of place. "Rome is subject to France," he grumbled; "but the Italians do not like it." If only these young women would keep away from politics and be content simply with dressing-up in pretty clothes. There was no pleasing Napoleon nowadays.

He was in fact as worried as he had ever been. His supremacy, which the Tsar had accepted at Tilsit in 1807 and still grudgingly conceded a year later at Erfurt, was now being openly challenged by the Russians, who were re-arming. As Napoleon's latest English biographer, Felix Markham, says: "Alexander's ukase of December 1810, which imposed high tariffs on French imports and opened his ports to neutral shipping, was a repudiation of the Continental System and convinced Napoleon that Russia was bent on war and a return to the English alliance." Though he had often declared that an invasion of Russia was a foolhardy undertaking, Napoleon determined to take the initiative and fixed June 1812 for the opening of the campaign.

On May 9 he left Paris for Germany to take charge. Pauline saw him go with bitterness mingled with anxiety. Her instinct told her that he was over-reaching himself. A small nagging sense of approaching doom was beginning to make itself felt. She had more definite reason to be bitter. She was desperately anxious about Canouville, who, as a Hussar commander, would be in the thick of the fighting in Russia. When the King of Naples arrived in Paris to join Napoleon as one of the major commanders in the campaign, she seized the opportunity to beg him to appoint Canouville to his staff, where, she hoped, he would be relatively secure behind the lines. Murat, always indulgent to his sister-in-law, at once agreed. Napoleon coldly countermanded the appointment.

It was an unhappy, ailing Pauline who left Paris early in June, heading for Aix-les-Bains. Madame Mère, on arrival at Aix towards the end of the month, was for once thoroughly alarmed by the state of her daughter's health. Napoleon's doctor, Corvisart, was summoned from Paris. Though he was familiar with Pauline's general condition, the remedies he prescribed were not effective. Pauline became worse and hardly moved from her bed or her day-bed. She rallied when Talma, the leading tragic actor of the day, arrived at Aix. She had met the tragedian in Paris the previous winter and was attracted to his exuberant personality. Talma, a vigorous fifty-year-old with a long line of gallantries behind him, had fallen head over heels in love with the coquettish, maladive princess. He found her even more adorable when, in early August, he saw her, pale and fragile, on her chaise-longue at Aix. Pauline was not one to repel such adoration. She rallied and seemed to recover her health. In later years Talma recalled with gratitude and affection the enchanted days they spent together. Poor Talma! His rôle was to restore

Pauline's spirits and, once this had happened, to open her eyes to more interesting possibilities than the adoration of an elderly actor.

Colonel Jean-Baptiste Duchand and Pauline were of an age. At thirty-one he had already made a name for himself as an artillery officer of outstanding dash and brilliance, and had been created a baron of the Empire. Wounded at the siege of Valencia the previous year, he had come to Aix-les-Bains to convalesce. He soon caught the attention of Pauline, with her penchant for young warriors. There was the additional amusement of playing the youthful colonel off against the ageing actor. Talma was in despair as the day approached, in the middle of September, when he had to leave to fulfil engagements at Lyon and the opening of the season in Paris. In the weeks that followed he bombarded Pauline with highly emotional declarations of affection. They remained unanswered or received a short formal acknowledgment. Pauline was too feeble in health, and too anxious about the war in Russia, to write love-letters. Though she seems not to have treated Duchand as more than one of many casual acquaintances, he had formed a deep and durable affection for her. This was to stand her in good stead in the difficult times ahead.

In May Napoleon, with Marie Louise at his side, was in Dresden, capital of the kingdom of Saxony, where his allies and vassals were assembled. It was, and was intended to be, a tremendous and dazzling demonstration of the might of the Napoleonic Empire. In June the vast force of French, Germans from the Confederation of the Rhine, Italians, Poles, Swiss and Dutch, with a few contingents from the Iberian peninsula, 600,000 in all, began the movement eastwards. On June 24 the first columns crossed the Niemen, where Napoleon had gone to assume personal command.

It took more than a fortnight for the news of the invasion of Russia to reach Aix-les-Bains, and as the Imperial forces drove deeper eastwards the intervals became longer. Pauline was too ill to worry overmuch, and of course she had faith in

Napoleon's invincibility. But she started cataloguing her jewellery and sent Michelot in Paris a continuous stream of injunctions on the need for economy in the upkeep of her houses. The news that reached Aix from the front was vaguely disturbing. Everyone had expected that before the French were far into Russian territory, the opposing armies would meet in a great battle in which Napoleon, as always, would prevail decisively, and then conclude a victor's peace. But as summer gave way to autumn the French had still not brought the enemy to battle and were advancing deeper and deeper into the illimitable wastes of Russia. There was an oppressive absence of activity, an ominous and incongruous calm not at all in the thunderous style of the conqueror.

The news from Spain was bad too. Wellington had pierced the French lines at Salamanca, and by mid-August the British were in Madrid. Pauline learned that Joseph had been forced to flee for his life. Napoleon was disappearing into the steppes. Her spirits revived with the news that Soult had reoccupied central Spain and Joseph was back in the palace at Madrid. But she continued to take her precautions. She instructed Michelot to send her the accounts for the upkeep of the park and the replacement of the linen at Neuilly, and once more emphasised the need for economy. If Prince Borghese arrived, his visit was not to lead to any expense falling on her.

Better news arrived from the Russian front. On September 7 the two armies had at last joined battle at Borodino. The French losses were frightful, but the Russians were in retreat and the road was open to Moscow, a week's march away. Then Pauline heard that Canouville had been killed in the battle. From a chain round his neck hung the miniature she had given him. A comrade-in-arms, recognising the portrait, had destroyed it in order to protect the Princess's reputation. She was inconsolable. She looked back on a long line of lovers and among them there were only two, Fréron and Canouville, who really counted. Once more Napoleon had wounded her cruelly. Had he not frustrated her plan to protect her beloved Canouville?

She left Aix-les-Bains at the end of October and, after resting
for a few days with her uncle the Cardinal in the Archbishop's
palace at Lyon, travelled by slow stages down to Marseille, ill
and in pain. She had decided to spend the winter at Hyères,
where Dr. Peyre came to join her. Horrified to find her in such
a lamentably low state of health, he was at a loss to do more than
prescribe rest and a light diet. Apart from her chronic internal
disorder, she was suffering from a deeper depression at this time
than at any stage in her life so far, due to the bitter blow of
Canouville's death, Napoleon's responsibility for his fate, and
her forebodings about the struggle in Russia.

The bulletins from Russia were more and more alarming.
Moscow, when the French entered it, was a deserted city, with
none of the stores they counted on. Instead of the hoped-for
overtures for peace, there was ominous silence from the Tsar.
Then came the news that the city had been burnt down, and
soon after that the French had started the long march home.
Heart-rending reports of the retreat trickled back to France—
the sudden onset of winter, the fearful toll of lives from exposure
and starvation, the ghastly passage of the Beresina river through
the floating ice, and finally, in December, the news that Napoleon
had left the emaciated remnant of the Grand Army and was
posting back to Paris. Pauline summoned her energies and told
Michelot to have a special cabinet made large enough to con-
tain all her jewels and to convert her holdings in State bonds
into jewellery. Jewellery in those troubled days increased in
value, and it was easily transportable. To help finance these
purchases she reduced the numbers and salaries of members of
her household.

In the New Year of 1813 she was still at Hyères. Napoleon,
to whom she had written, told her, in his usual crisp manner:
"You would have done better to come to Paris rather than
wander from place to place hoping for something from the
doctors. You would have done better to go to Nice rather than
Hyères. I see no objection to your going to Nice."

Pauline had no intention of returning to Paris. She did not

feel up to undertaking the long journey across France. The idea of Nice smiled on her, and she spent the winter there. She may have felt safer in the south of France. Despite her forebodings, she retained her faith in Napoleon's extraordinary capacities and rejoiced to hear that Paris was quiet and that the Emperor was about to take the field once again, with a new army raised from the inexhaustible man-power of France. By April he was across the Rhine. At first all went well. The Russians and Prussians were defeated at Lutzen on May 2 and again at Bautzen three weeks later. During the armistice that followed Napoleon, who was at Dresden, received the news that Wellington had beaten the French at Vittoria on June 21. This was the end of the French occupation of Spain.

Pauline had left Nice at the end of May to go to Gréoux-les-Bains, the watering-place near Aix-en-Provence where she had been sent when seriously ill in 1807. It had been a long and uncomfortable journey, by boat from Nice to Fréjus and then by slow stages over hilly country by carriage and the sedan-chair she preferred. The news from Spain threw her into the depths of depression. Poor Joseph, he had abandoned his travelling carriage and galloped from Madrid to the frontier, arriving at St. Jean de Luz with only a single coin in his pocket. Worse was to come. After fruitless discussions between Napoleon and Metternich during the summer of 1813, war broke out again in Eastern Europe on August 10. Outnumbered, for almost all Europe was against him, including Sweden under the Crown Prince (once one of Napoleon's leading marshals, Bernadotte), and for once outmanoeuvred, for the wary allies contrived to fight the individual commanders rather than the Emperor himself, Napoleon finally came face to face with the Allies at Leipzig. There, in two days' bitter fighting on October 17 and 18, 1813, the French were broken, and on the 20th Napoleon retreated across the Rhine with barely seventy thousand men.

From her day-bed at Gréoux Pauline followed the progress of the German campaign and listened to the rumblings of disaster. From all that had gone before it might have been expected that she would have concentrated on looking after her own interests, perhaps made plans to leave France, or even seen in the fate which was overtaking her brother a requital of all the injustices she felt she had suffered from him over the years. On the contrary, all that was best in her character asserted itself at this moment of crisis in the family fortunes. She sent stern instructions to her household in Paris not to breathe or write a word about political matters. She sold a valuable necklace she had recently acquired as part of her policy of turning her assets into portable valuables, and, with another 100,000 francs of ready money, assembled 300,000 francs which she offered to Napoleon several days before the final defeat at Leipzig. After the battle Napoleon wrote, rather grandly, that he accepted the gift, but believed that the goodwill and resources of "my peoples" were such that he could count on being able to meet the enormous expenses which would be involved in the campaigns of 1814 and 1815. Pauline's letters to her mother's man of business in Paris (Decazes, the future minister of Louis XVIII) made it clear that she had offered this large sum to Napoleon out of a sense of duty ("*J'ai fait ce que je dois*"), and was desperately anxious about her own financial position and the safeguarding of her jewellery. The remarkable thing is that the self-centred and ailing Pauline should have risen so munificently to the occasion. Beneath the frivolity there lay a bedrock of loyalty to the clan and a sense of occasion.

The strain was almost too great, and that winter Pauline nearly died. On doctor's advice she left Gréoux in November for Nice, too ill to respond to Madame Mère's pressing appeals to her to come to Paris. She recovered sufficiently in the New Year to give instructions for further drastic reductions in the expenses of her household.

The New Year of 1814 opened with ominous calm, and then the fateful news reached Nice that a vast army of Austrians, Prussians and Russians had crossed the Rhine and were advancing unopposed across northern and eastern France. Pauline sent one of her ladies to Paris while there was time with instructions to collect all her jewels, which had been stored in various safe places, and give them to Madame Mère, with any available loose cash.

The Allies were driving for Paris in two great columns. By the end of January Blücher's northern column of Prussians and Russians had reached the Marne, and the southerly column of Austrians, under the supreme commander, Schwarzenberg, were on the Seine. The Emperor of Austria, the Tsar of Russia and the King of Prussia accompanied the armies. In Nice Napoleon's sister waited breathlessly to see what he would do. What an unspeakable relief to hear that he had twice driven the Prussians and Russians back, and a few days later completely routed them, at Champaubert and Montmirail. Napoleon then shifted rapidly from the valley of the Marne, where these engagements had taken place, to the valley of the Seine, where Schwarzenberg and his Austrians were moving dangerously close to Paris. In five days of fighting at Nangis and Montereau he drove the Austrians back as far as Troyes.

Napoleon might have been able, had he wished, to conclude an honourable peace after these brilliant manœuvrings which had re-emphasised his military superiority over the invading Allies. Fighting against odds, he had shown that he could still run rings round any commander in Europe. But Napoleon fought only to win, not to make peace, and the moment of opportunity passed, for even Napoleon could not win without tools, and the tools were breaking in his hands. The conscripts were deserting, there was a shortage of muskets, guns and other supplies. The Allies, on their side, were determined to finish the job. It did not take long to do it. On March 9 Napoleon was defeated by Blücher at Laon, and retreated to Rheims. At Arcis-sur-Aube ten days later he was soundly beaten by Schwarzenberg. It seemed to be the end. Yet he made a last desperate throw. Instead of falling back on Paris, he moved to the Rhine fortresses where he could threaten the Allied lines of communication. The threat, he hoped, would draw them back from the capital, but the bluff did not work. Schwarzenberg pushed on to Paris, effected a junction with Blücher at Meaux, and on March 29 was outside the capital. Leaving his army, Napoleon rushed to Fontainebleau, still full of fight. When he reached the château on the 30th he was greeted with the news that Paris had capitulated. On April 4 he abdicated.

Pauline by this time was at the Château de Bouillidou, near Le Luc, in the hinterland north of Hyères. She heard that Napoleon would be passing through Le Luc on the way to the coast and exile in Elba. She determined to wait and see him, though her brother-in-law Bacciochi, writing from Marseille, where he and Elisa had fled from their principality of Lucca, urged her to come with him to Rome and safety. Various other members of the family were hastening to leave France for places of refuge. Madame Mère and her brother the Cardinal were on their way from Lyons to Rome. Jérôme and Joseph were planning to escape to America. Lucien was already in England. Pauline kept calm. She rejected Bacciochi's offer with scorn. "As the Emperor will be passing through," she replied, "I want to see him and offer him my sympathy. If he agrees that I should accompany him I will not leave his side. If he does not want it, I will go to Naples and stay with the King of Naples. I did not love the Emperor as a sovereign, but I loved him as a brother and I will remain faithful to him till death." Several biographers make out that Pauline had not heard of the abdication until the Commissioners escorting him informed her minutes before Napoleon arrived at the Château de Bouillidou; but it is clear from this letter to Bacciochi dated April 21, 1814, that she had already heard the news by that date, five days before Napoleon's arrival.

On April 26, the advance guard of officials of the Allied Powers who were escorting the fallen Emperor presented themselves at the château. Pauline tried to get up from her couch but was too ill and too upset to make the effort. Outside, the shouts and curses of the mob following the cortège grew louder. The Emperor was approaching. Leaping down from his carriage, he was surprised not to see his sister in the doorway. Monsieur de Montbreton, Pauline's equerry, was equally surprised. He did not recognise as the Emperor the strangely dressed man who now rushed into the house. From her couch Pauline instinctively stretched out her arms in welcome, but instead of the familiar figure in the long grey greatcoat over the severe plain tunic and white breeches of the Guard, she saw a man in fancy dress. She drew back in surprise, and looked more intently.

"What is that uniform you are wearing?" she cried, and burst into tears.

She recognised the uniform as that of an Austrian general. Yes, and over it Napoleon was wearing a Russian cloak and under his arm held a Prussian képi. It is not recorded what article of apparel was contributed by Colonel Sir Neil Campbell, who was to go with him to Elba as British Commissioner.

"Pauline," he said stiffly, "would you have liked to see me dead?"

He had felt ridiculous when the Commissioners had stopped the carriage as the mob surged round them near the château and persuaded him, for his own safety, to accept a uniform from one, a cloak from another, a cap from a third. Now he felt thoroughly ashamed as he heard Pauline saying: "I cannot possibly embrace you wearing an enemy uniform. Oh, Napoleon, what have you done!"

Glowering, Napoleon turned on his heel, strode to an adjoining room, and reappeared a few minutes later wearing a French Guards uniform.

Pauline was trembling uncontrollably as she held him in her arms, prey to an unusual mixture of emotions. It was as if she was mothering him, as if he was a small boy who had been forgiven after disgracing himself. For the first time she had seen the Emperor without dignity, his nerve gone, ready to hide and run from his persecutors. This revelation of weakness was shattering. Yet she had never loved Napoleon so much, as she smoothed his matted hair and stroked his mud-bespattered cheek. The scene had been observed by Neil Campbell, who noted that on his journey to Elba, amid the hostility of the populace and in evident fear of his life, Napoleon "certainly exhibited more timidity than one would have expected from a man of his calibre".

Pauline made over the château to Napoleon and his escort and went to stay in the neighbourhood. They spent the night there, and the next day she told him she was ready to come with him at once to Elba. He preferred her to wait. So Pauline, a little disconcerted, decided to accept her brother-in-law Murat's invitation to go to Naples.

Before leaving France she wanted to see Duchand again, not for any personal reason but because he had impressed her as a businessman. He adored Pauline and came to Bouillidou in mid-May. She was confirmed in her first impression. Here was a man, devoted not only to herself but to the Emperor, on whom she could rely in troubled times. Belonging to a family of financiers from Grenoble, he had a business sense. He gave her the utmost confidence. When he returned to Paris a fortnight later Duchand carried a letter of introduction to Michelot. In it Pauline told her *intendant* that she had complete confidence in Duchand, who would explain orally the business arrangements they had talked over, and return to report to her in Italy when everything was in order.

Greatly relieved to feel that her affairs were in good hands, she made plans to leave for Naples. In late May she travelled to Fréius to board the frigate which the King of Naples had sent to fetch her. On the way, on June 1, 1814, she called at Porto Ferraio and spent the night there. She found Napoleon not best pleased, since Murat, anxious to keep his throne, had deserted the Empire at the climax of the struggle, and was thus a traitor in his eyes. It was a doleful visit, and she was deeply moved to see her brother so humiliated and yet so proud in his little island. She promised faithfully to come and spend the winter with him, and—a characteristic gesture—bought a plot of land near the capital to demonstrate her stake in his new dominion, and at the same time satisfy her business instincts which suggested that Napoleon's arrival would send up land values in Elba.

18. Elba and the Hundred Days
1814-15

MURAT'S CONDUCT HAD CERTAINLY BEEN OPPORTUNIST. After the Russian disaster he had been in contact secretly with the Austrians, hoping to promote a peace settlement and save his throne. After Leipzig, where he had played his part brilliantly in command of the French right wing, he saw that Napoleon was irretrievably ruined. Rushing back to his capital immediately after the battle, he tried vainly to persuade Napoleon to make him king of a united Italy. On Napoleon refusing, he signed a treaty of alliance with Austria on January 11, 1814. By Napoleon's refusal the cause of Italian unity had been put back for fifty years, and Murat, had he known it, had signed his own death warrant. For another twelve months he was able to hold his uneasy throne.

Pauline wrote to her mother about this time criticising Elisa for having gone to the Habsburg court at Vienna and for thinking of going to live in Paris. It would be an unpardonable betrayal for any member of the family to live in France under the Bourbons. The Emperor himself had said so. She hoped Joseph would go and see the Emperor in Elba. He should not be left alone at a moment like this. Yet she had no word of reproach for Murat. She had always been fond of this brother-in-law, whose warm-heartedness and bravery in battle evidently made him an exception to her general conviction that all members of the family owed absolute loyalty to Napoleon in misfortune.

When she drew into port on that brilliant, hot June day in 1814 and saw the King of Naples waiting to receive her in state at the quayside, her feeling was one of gratitude. His imposing soldierly figure inspired her with confidence. Under Murat's protection she could rest, recover her health, and set her private affairs in order. She was enchanted by the Villa Favorita he had put at her disposal by the sea at Portici, near Herculaneum. She wrote long letters to Lucien and Madame Mère, who were in Rome. "My health is still bad," she told Lucien, "but my doctors hold out the hope of recovery if I follow a régime, and particularly if I take baths. I need rest, I have suffered so much." She wanted to know when Madame Mère intended to go to Elba. She planned to go herself, she had promised the Emperor to spend the winter with him.

During the next four months she lived at La Favorita, apart from a few weeks which she spent during the heat of the summer at Vomero in the cooler hilly ground on the other side of Naples. She looked after her health and her business affairs, especially her considerable real estate in France. There could be no certainty that the Bourbons would honour their obligations to the Bona-partes under the Treaty of Fontainebleau. Her brother was already finding that he was not receiving the agreed sums with which to maintain his miniature court in Elba and pay the salaries of his veterans. There was evidently every risk of the Bonaparte family properties being confiscated. Fortunately she had Michelot in Paris, with Duchand to help. She sent imperative instructions to Michelot to sell the Hôtel de Charost and the Château de Neuilly as quickly as possible, and to dispatch ornaments and furniture from the two houses to Naples.

She did not succeed in selling Neuilly; as anticipated, it was annexed by Louis XVIII, who disposed of it to the Duc d'Orléans in 1820 in exchange for a valuable Orléans property. She was more fortunate with the Hôtel de Charost. The Duke of Wellington, his military career apparently terminated with his triumphs over the French in Spain and Napoleon's abdication in April 1814, had been offered the post of Ambassador to France. The Duke spent a few days in Paris in May, and saw the house. The Emperor of Austria, in Paris with the Allied occupation forces, had just vacated it. The Duke liked it, but regretfully concluded that it was too large. To assure British representation with Louis XVIII after the Treaty of Peace signed on May 30, Sir Charles Stuart had been appointed British Minister on June 4, 1814. To him the Duke wrote from London in July:

"The Prince Borghese's house is so very large that, however much I wish to have it, as thinking it the only house that I have seen that would perfectly answer, I feel a great disinclination to apply to the government to purchase it. I must therefore give up all thought of it."

Michelot meanwhile had not been idle. Sir Charles Stuart acted energetically. An English resident, Quentin Craufurd, a well-known dilettante, was eager to help. When the Duke arrived as Ambassador on August 22, 1814, Stuart was able to report that the Hôtel de Charost and its contents could be had for 800,000 francs (about £224,000, 1964), 50,000 francs less than Michelot's original price, plus another 63,000 francs for the separate stables in the rue d'Anjou—at present the garage of the British Embassy. The Duke moved in at once. His mission accomplished, Charles Stuart left Paris on August 24. On August 26 the Duke signed the inventory of contents. On August 29 he firmly told the Under-Secretary at the Foreign Office that he had "come into the house, having determined on purchase from what passed on the subject in London." The Prince Regent warmly approved the transaction.

Wellington spent only four months as Ambassador in Paris, during which time he entered with zest into the social and political life of the capital. The Duchess of Wellington inevitably became one of the customers of Leroy, whose accounts show that she bought from him a number of regulation mantillas for use at the court of Louis XVIII. The Duke was cheered when he rode in the streets, hunted with the royal family, attended Madame Récamier's salon and became firm friends with Madame de Staël, of whom he later recorded: "I have said to her more than once: *'Je déteste parler politique,'* and she answered: *'Parler politique pour moi c'est vivre.'* " On January 24, 1815, he left for Vienna to relieve Castlereagh as first British plenipotentiary at the Congress which had been sitting since the previous September, and was succeeded as Ambassador by Sir Charles Stuart (who stayed in Paris for nearly ten years).

Soon after she reached Elba Pauline had word from Michelot that he and the Duke had at last (on October 24, 1814) signed the contract of sale, which provided for payments in instalments ending in August, 1816. The first instalment for the value of half the contents was paid immediately, all instalments on the house and contents were completed by the agreed date. These payments from the British Government, apart from ornaments and furniture sent to Italy and such of her jewellery as Madame Mère had been able to bring out of France, were now her chief means of livelihood. By the end of 1814 the Bourbons, as she expected, had confiscated all Bonaparte property in France. She ceased to enjoy the revenues of the duchy of Guastalla on the Empress Marie Louise becoming Duchess of Parma.

Through dread of sea-sickness Pauline put off her departure for Elba from day to day. At last, on October 29, 1814, Napoleon's brig, the *Inconstant*, the one naval vessel allowed him under the Treaty of Fontainebleau, was brought down from Baiae to her villa at Portici, and she went on board. After a stop at Leghorn, the travellers reached Porto Ferraio on November 1. Napoleon received her on the quayside from which the Elban flag was waving, a white flag with a band of orange and three large bees, with cannon saluting, a guard of honour, and his little court around him. He was delighted to welcome her, and she fell rapturously into his arms.

These past five months had hardly been gay for Napoleon. He had made an effort to reconcile himself with his fate. He had examined his career, assessed his contribution to history, admitted faults. "Those who blame me have never drunk of Fortune's intoxicating cup." He had burnt off his flaming energy by organising and galvanising his diminutive island empire.

Under the terms of the Treaty of Fontainebleau Napoleon retained his title and rank of Emperor and received the sovereignty of Elba. The island was thus his to do with as he pleased. With the revenue from the iron and salt mines, from the tunny fisheries and from customs and indirect taxation, and counting on the substantial annual income granted under the treaty, he set out to maintain a considerable establishment. Most of the four million francs he had brought with him from Fontainebleau had been pilfered en route. There were the seven hundred men of the Old Guard who had been allowed to accompany him, thirty Polish cavalrymen, an Elban militia of some eight hundred men, and the *Inconstant*, as well as a numerous staff of court officials and household servants. The establishment was too heavy for the budget, even before it became apparent that the restored régime in Paris had no intention of paying a single franc of the agreed allowance.

A careful record of Napoleon's activities in Elba was kept by his valet, Louis Joseph Narcisse Marchand. Marchand's mother had been appointed one of the three nurses in attendance on the King of Rome (whom she followed to Vienna after the abdication), and young Louis, at the age of twenty, had entered the Imperial household as page in 1811. At the abdication Constant and Rustam deserted their master and Marchand was selected as first valet. He stayed to the end with Napoleon, who on his death-bed recognised this fidelity by making him a count of the Empire.

Marchand says that Napoleon, the moment he landed, immediately inspected the public buildings at Porto Ferraio, toured the island and visited the mines. Selecting as his residence a fine house, I Mulini, half-way up the ridge above the harbour, he decided that it must be enlarged. It was too small to accommodate the Empress and the King of Rome, as well as Pauline. The work was immediately started. Napoleon went to live at the Mairie and, with the onset of the summer heat, often spent the night in the Hermitage of the Madonna at Marciana Alta on the high slopes of Monte Campana. On the property on the slopes of Monte San Martino about four miles south-west of Porto Ferraio which Pauline had acquired on impulse during her first short visit to Elba, he decided to build a simple villa. He amused himself by having the main reception room decorated in the Egyptian style (always the hankering after the East) by artists who came over from the Italian mainland, and by constructing a modern bathroom with Pompeian frescoes. "Everything," says Marchand, "had to be created at Elba." Roads began to radiate from Porto Ferraio across the island. A new street was built to give easy access to the little palace of I Mulini. The streets of Porto Ferraio were widened and proper town drainage installed. A municipal theatre was constructed. Fortifications were strengthened and new ones built. Neil Campbell had never seen a man of such restless energy.

Having a vivid recollection from her visit in May of the shabby buildings and dirty narrow streets of Porto Ferraio, Pauline was amazed by the sparkling changes. This, she knew, must be the result of Napoleon's driving energy. At least he had found ways to occupy himself. But what a pathetic little stage for the man who had dominated the European amphitheatre, how pathetic she realised from the half eager, half apologetic way he drove her about the island to view the new roads and buildings she dutifully admired.

She understood how close the iron will had come to cracking during those days of final defeat. She knew that he had tried to poison himself at Fontainebleau the night that he had read the humiliating terms presented by the victorious Allies. She remembered the remark he had made after his attendants forced emetics down his throat and he gradually revived in the cool of the breaking dawn: "I must live and await all that Providence has in store for me." She understood how he missed not only the pace and challenge of power but all that went with it in terms of human relationships. Gone were the ministers and generals, the secretaries and chamberlains, all the dynamic human apparatus of government, conquest and ostentation. Gone the progresses from the Tuileries to Fontainebleau, St. Cloud or Compiègne, or further afield to Dresden or some other capital to receive the homage of subject princes, or to Erfurt or Tilsit to decide the fate of the world with the Tsar. Now there was only a charming small palace in a miniature capital, a villa in the hills and a hermitage in the forest. The functionaries were there, but only to administer a tiny court. There were men to take orders, but only such as an owner of a large estate might need to issue. A supreme commander used to commanding a quarter of a million men now concerned himself with a few hundred Guards and the Elba militia. Except for an occasional visitor from abroad, the only foreign potentate with whom he conversed was the amiable Sir Neil Campbell.

Pauline sensed that he even missed the more or less continuous rows he had had throughout his reign with the members of the family. This subdued and grateful Napoleon who seemed so glad to see her was very different from the imperious leader who had expected his sisters and brothers to do exactly what they were told and raged if his instructions were not carried out. He had been genuinely pleased when Madame Mère had come to live at Elba, but it could not be pretended that she was lively company. Pauline went at once to see her mother in the spacious villa, the Casa Vantini, close to I Mulini, which Napoleon had equipped for her, and seeing her there with her father confessor, Pauline realised that Signora Letizia had, so to speak, gone back to the period before the days of unwanted greatness. Elba was welcomed as a final refuge, she was as content as if she were back in her native Ajaccio, and here as there everybody spoke Italian.

How, Pauline wondered, could Napoleon live, a virtual widower? She heard that his glance fell from time to time on the wives of officers of the garrison. But these were passing fancies. Did he really expect Marie Louise to come back to him, bringing their son? What of Marie Walewska who, Pauline knew, had visited the island secretly during the summer? How inexpressibly sad was the truth as she learned it.

There had been a moment, soon after his abdication, when he had been tempted to seek happiness where he was certain of finding it. Marie Walewska had written to him affectionately, telling him she was going to take the baths of Lucca that autumn.

"If you go to the baths of Lucca," he replied on April 15, "I would be very glad to see you and your son. Never doubt me."

Marie arrived at Elba late at night on September 1, with her son, her younger sister and her brother, Colonel Leczinski. Napoleon, to escape the heat, was living at the Hermitage of the Madonna. At the port a carriage was waiting for the two ladies and the little boy, and a horse for Colonel Leczinski. When they reached the Hermitage they descried Napoleon in the dappled moonlight, standing in the chestnut wood surrounding the Hermitage. The upper floor of the building consisted of a chapel, cared for by two recluses who lived in the cellar. This left four small communicating rooms free for the Emperor's use. Napoleon escorted his guests into this simple suite, bade them make themselves at home, and went off to sleep in a tent in the wood which he had erected for himself and two menservants. The next day Marie and her relations left. It is doubtful whether she and Napoleon were ever alone during her brief visit, which he did his best to keep secret.

He had reasons for particular discretion. He continued to hope that Marie Louise and his son would join him in Elba. Her letters immediately after his fall gave him reason to believe she loved him and was trying to come, but although her letters to Napoleon suggest that she was genuinely in love with him, she was never to see him again. Marie Louise had been led to expect before the marriage that she was being sacrificed, for reasons of state, to a monster. The monster proved to be a passionate lover, a considerate husband who tried, after his own peculiar fashion, to amuse his young wife, whether by arranging magnificent balls and festivities which bored him, or spending hours teaching her to ride. Marie Louise fell in love with her monster. Her affection was assured when she knew that, at the moment of terror and agony, he had told the doctors to save her and sacrifice the child. She wanted to join Napoleon in exile, and bring their son with her. During the summer of 1814 many letters were exchanged between General Bertrand, the head of

Napoleon's household, and Méneval, whom Napoleon had attached to Marie Louise when she went to Vienna after the abdication. It was expected at Porto Ferraio that Marie Louise would find it easy to pay frequent visits to Elba from Parma, capital of her duchy.

But Marie Louise, before going to Parma and afterwards as she hoped to Elba, decided to take the cure at Aix-les-Bains. On arrival at Aix she found that Prince Nicolas Esterhazy, the elderly retiring personage whom the Austrian Government had attached to her as political adviser, had been replaced by General Count Neipperg. "Count Neipperg," Méneval records, "was not particularly well-favoured. A black bandage covered the deep cicatrice of a wound by which he had lost an eye, but . . . this wound rather suited the ensemble of his face, which had a martial character. His hair was of a light blonde colour, scanty and curly. His glance was bright and penetrating . . . He was of middle height and well-built, and the elegance of his figure was heightened by the loose cut of his Hungarian uniform. General Neipperg was at that time about forty-two years old."

Metternich had chosen his man well. Pauline, sensitive to martial valour and easily captivated by a well-cut uniform, would not have resisted this forty-two-year-old warrior as versed in the lists of love as of war. Marie Louise's sensual nature was not proof for long. Neipperg was accurate when he wrote to his Italian mistress (or so Méneval recorded): "I hope to be on the most intimate terms with her before six months are out, and soon to be her husband." She became his lover that autumn, had two children by him during Napoleon's life-time, and married him after the Emperor's death.

Napoleon guessed what was happening. "My wife no longer writes to me," he said on September 20. "My son is snatched away from me. No such barbarous act is recorded in modern times." Joséphine had died at Malmaison on May 29. She, at least, had not wanted to live after his downfall; Joséphine who, "after all is said and done," he was to tell them at St. Helena, "gave her husband happiness and was always his tenderest friend, always and in all events showing submission, devotion, absolute self-sacrifice. I have always thought of her with tender affection and keen gratitude."

Joséphine dead, Marie Louise faithless, Marie Walewska remote and unattainable: Napoleon brooded on his loneliness and was thankful to see Pauline, the one of all the family for whom he had felt tenderness, however harshly he had been constrained to try to order her life. Pauline was sympathetic, uncomplicated, with a zest for simple and elemental pleasures. He looked to her to bring some light and colour into the drab life of provincial Porto Ferraio.

She was charmed by the aspect of the renovated palace with its plain white front and green shutters, with the garden, its grass newly sown and flowers freshly planted, looking out over the harbour. The enlargements and redecorations had been completed in record time. Napoleon had taken over the ground floor for his own private apartments and offices for his staff and above it had built a single large salon which could serve for receptions or as a ball-room. One wing had been adapted to accommodate the kitchens and household rooms, the other contained a large salon which was used for theatrical performances and could be partitioned so as to serve as a dining-room. On the floor above were the apartments he had designed for the Empress and the King of Rome. Marie Louise and their son, he now knew, would never inhabit them, and it was in these rooms that Pauline went to live.

The arrival of Pauline in Elba revived the old stories about her relations with Napoleon. Gossip was rife in Paris and London. It was fed by Bourbon spies in the island, and Pauline's correspondence with Madame Michelot, wife of her *intendant*, and with Duchand, who had become her financial adviser, was intercepted and tampered with. Damaging passages were forged and inserted in innocent business letters. The responsibility of Talleyrand is heavy in this murky affair; he made it his business to feed the insatiable appetite of Louis XVIII for discreditable stories about Napoleon and his family. Napoleon was shown some of these doctored letters in Paris during the Hundred Days and has recorded his indignation. All responsible modern commentators have dismissed the myth of an unnatural relationship between Napoleon and Pauline. When their highly individual temperaments were not driving them into irritation or resentment, brother and sister were capable of deep affection for each other, but nothing more.

Pauline set to work with a will to organise her brother's life. It was apparent to her that what he needed was the reconstruction of the routine to which he had become accustomed, even though it were the mere illusion of the reality. So she instituted daily receptions at which the local worthies came to pay their respects, balls and concerts several times a week, and afternoon expeditions and picnics. Sometimes they spent the evening quietly with Madame Mère. Under Pauline's skilful touch and gay personality the dreary provincial round preened itself and flaunted the plumage of a court, a miniature court, but one of which one man was the centre. The Emperor felt better. He began to recover his habits of imperious irritation. Pauline was delighted, even when she was the victim of some scathing sally about the inappropriateness of her toilette at dinner. She smiled indulgently when Napoleon refused to pay a bill for sixty-two francs thirty centimes for sunblinds for her apartments: "As this expense was not authorised, the Princess will pay." Napoleon was himself again. For the first time in her life Pauline forgot herself in her concern for somebody else. We hear no word of her being ill during the months she spent on Elba. However, the discomfort she had experienced for many years would never be cured, and Marchand noticed that she was carried down in a chair from her apartments every evening, and preferred to sit in a sedan-chair on expeditions in the island rather than riding in a carriage. For him this princess was the perfection of beauty, and he loved to watch her smiling and talking gaily from her sedan-chair with the group of young officers who always accompanied her.

On February 16, 1815, Pauline addressed to the British

Commander an invitation to a ball she was planning to give at the end of the month. Sir Neil Campbell replied that he would be unable to come as he would be absent in Leghorn at that time. Napoleon pricked up his ears when this was reported to him.

He had been intently watching the proceedings of the Congress of Vienna and the state of affairs in Europe. The victorious Allies were divided on the settlement of Europe, there was unrest in the Low Countries where the Belgians were outraged at the idea of being placed under Dutch rule, the Tsar had designs on Poland, the Prussians wanted to swallow up Saxony, the Italians, who had tasted unity under Napoleon, were in a ferment when they heard that the Habsburgs were coming to settle back into their former Italian fiefs. In France itself there were rumblings of discontent. The thousands of soldiers of the Napoleonic armies, now disbanded, grumbled at their shabby treatment under the Bourbons, and pined for the days of glory under the Emperor. The peasants, especially those who had been living on lands confiscated during the revolution, were uneasy. The Bourbons lacked the style of the Empire.

Lord John Russell, visiting Napoleon in December, was sure he was meditating some great stroke. Under the Treaty of Fontainebleau he should have received two million francs a year from Louis XVIII; nothing was ever paid, despite the reproaches of Pauline to Campbell and of British statesmen to Talleyrand. His wife and child were being kept from him. Disturbing reports reached him that the Bourbon government in Paris were planning to remove him to the Azores, the West Indies or St. Helena. He determined to break out of this ridiculous and dangerous confinement and he coolly awaited his moment to escape, to recover, to avenge himself.

The moment came in February with the conjuncture of two vital items of news—reports of a plot in Paris by the arch-intriguer Fouché to overthrow the Bourbons, and the unguarded announcement by Neil Campbell of his intention to be absent from the island. Pauline was not taken into her brother's confidence. It was not till the morning of Sunday, February 26, that she became aware of what was afoot. The whole island, indeed, must have seen that Napoleon was about to leave. The *Inconstant* was brought into harbour, with six smaller vessels. His private army, 1,050 officers and men, were under orders to sail. Ammunition, stores and baggage were loaded. Napoleon solemnly went to church in the morning, and afterwards reviewed his troops, who then proceeded to the ships. He received deputations from the townspeople, who begged him not to leave them. It remains a mystery why the Allied authorities in the island, even though the British Commissioner was away, showed themselves completely indifferent to these very overt preparations for departure.

Madame Mère, Pauline, Comtesse Bertrand and several wives of the staff, Marchand records, were to stay behind in the island and "await developments". It evidently did not occur to Napoleon that by leaving his mother and sister virtually without protection on Elba he was placing them in peril of capture or worse. Affection, prudence, the ordinary sentiments counted for nothing when it was a question of his destiny. Madame Mère understood. Napoleon confided his plans to her one evening in late February in the garden of I Mulini, forbidding her to speak of them even to Pauline. She bade him go and fulfil his destiny. As soon as she heard that he had eluded the British patrols and landed in France, she wrote in triumph to Lucien to inform him of "the departure from this town of our dear Emperor and his arrival at Golfe Juan . . . The Emperor is well and I am overjoyed." Determined to wait in Elba for news, it was not till she heard that France practically to a man was rallying to the Emperor that she decided to leave for France via Naples in the ship of the line that her son-in-law Murat had sent to escort her.

Nobody, not even Madame Mère, had been prouder than Pauline of Napoleon in the days of his glory. She would have been the first to applaud his bid to regain his throne if she believed it feasible. It did not occur to her to worry about her own safety or complain that she and her mother were being deserted. She simply felt that the bid was doomed to failure, and her heart sank. It seemed inconceivable to her that Napoleon with his thousand men could pit himself against the whole of Europe. During the afternoon she went to see him. Silently she offered him her finest diamond necklace. He accepted the gift, worth half a million francs, casually, and asked her to hand the diamonds to Marchand, who, preparatory to leaving with Napoleon, was packing in the adjoining room two uniforms and some shirts which the Emperor had told him were all he wanted.

"Here," she said, her pretty face swollen with crying, "the Emperor might have need of this. If that unfortunately were to be the case, Marchand, never abandon him. Take good care of him. Adieu." She gave Marchand her hand to kiss.

Marchand tried to console her. "Everything makes me hope it is 'au revoir', Your Highness."

"That is not what I think," she murmured miserably. Napoleon came in at that moment, and took Pauline out into the garden to console and encourage her.

Later in the afternoon Napoleon said goodbye to the Signora and Pauline. At seven he drove down to the port, and at eight boarded the *Inconstant*. At nine o'clock the little squadron weighed for France. The sequel, for Pauline, was a disagreeable scene with Sir Neil, who returned from his excursion two days later.

"Your brother has violated his parole," he shouted. "But the Mediterranean is full of our ships and at this very moment he is surely in our hands." Concealing her agitation, she reproved him coldly for shouting at her.

The streets and squares of Porto Ferraio, so lately humming with activity, were silent and hushed, as if the inhabitants were in mourning for the departed Captain around whom all had revolved. The palazzetto echoed with emptiness. She was alone with Madame Mère. She wished she could share her mother's indomitable optimism, but knew in her heart of hearts that she would never see Napoleon again. At least he had her diamonds.

She was not to know that they were to be found by the English in his travelling coach at Waterloo.

One French officer, inadvertently left behind on distant guard duty, remained in Elba. To Lieutenant Monier Pauline appealed for help to arrange for her to cross to the mainland. She could not bear the prospect of sharing Elba with the grumpy British Commissioner and determined to leave as soon as she could. Though she foresaw no particular danger, she did not care for the idea of leaving her mother behind, but Signora Letizia repeated firmly that she intended to stay in Elba for the present and then join the Emperor in France. During the night of March 3-4 a distracted and heavy-hearted Pauline sailed in an open boat for Viareggio, taking with her Monier, her single lady-in-waiting and four servants. Near Viareggio, where they arrived the following afternoon, her sister Elisa possessed a property, the Château of Campignano sul Monte, which she had acquired when Hereditary Princess of Piombino. Elisa herself was in Bologna, and the château was shut. But Elisa's bailiff was willing to open it, and at Campignano Pauline and her small suite thankfully installed themselves.

They were not left long in peace. With the overthrow of the Napoleonic Empire in 1814, the Austrians had re-established possession of their former territories in Italy. The arrival of one of the escaped Emperor's sisters in the residence of another of the sisters seemed to the Austrian Governor an outrage, although the Emperor of Austria had personally restored to Elisa her various possessions in Italy. But this was before Napoleon had escaped from Elba. The Governor sent a troop of cavalry to the château with instructions that Pauline and her sister were to be kept incommunicado. Pauline was to all effects a state prisoner. Elisa was arrested and imprisoned at Brünn in Moravia.

The Governor could hardly have known at this time that Napoleon had landed at Golfe Juan near Cannes and was on his way through France to Paris. Had he done so, he would not have been deterred. As soon as the news of the escape and landing was known, the Allies, who were still in session at

Vienna, declared on March 13 that Napoleon had placed himself outside the bounds of civil and social relations and was "consigned to public justice as an enemy and disturber of the peace of the world".

The driblets of news that trickled through to Pauline under surveillance at Campignano lifted her spirits from time to time. Her brother had resumed his throne on March 20. The Bourbons were in flight again. The French people had welcomed the Emperor home with delirium. Yet Pauline could not overcome a dull aching feeling of desolation. Least politically minded of the Bonapartes, her instincts were sure. The Family, she was certain, was doomed. Even Napoleon with the French people behind him would not be able to break out of this relentless ring of destruction she felt to be closing in.

Her situation became more and more deplorable as time went on. She sent Monier to Paris to report to Napoleon. Napoleon sternly called on the Grand Duke of Tuscany to set her at liberty, and ordered a frigate to be sent to Leghorn to bring her to France. The Grand Duke paid no attention and Napoleon's orders in regard to the naval vessel were not carried out. Napoleon, alas, was no longer the master of Europe. Pauline knew this, but was grateful to him.

From Naples, Murat and Caroline interceded in vain with the Austrian authorities. The unfortunate King of Naples was regarded by the Allies as an adversary and by Napoleon as a poltroon. In his desperate position he fought his last battle, at Tolentino on May 3, threw up his kingdom of Naples and fled in disguise to Toulon, where he offered his allegiance to Napoleon, who rejected the offer.

Hating her imprisonment and fearing worse—a fortress in Graz or Brünn—Pauline, not for the first time, succeeded in achieving a change of place by "making herself ill". Soon she really became seriously ill, and contrived to have this attested by leading doctors from Lucca. Throughout this strange twilight period of the Hundred Days, the distracted members of the Bonaparte family, except Napoleon himself and Murat, could still count on a certain minimum of consideration due to an Imperial house from the established monarchies. Caroline, Murat's wife, was allowed to live peacefully in Trieste, where Elisa was eventually permitted to join her. Rome, under Pius VII, was a haven for any of them who cared to go there. On June 5 Pauline received permission to go to Lucca to take the cure. She set out the next day, with an escort of twenty Austrian soldiers.

It was a wonderful relief, and soon she felt restored. She was short of money, but Napoleon, on his return to Paris, had personally arranged for a large sum, sequestered after the first abdication, to be restored to her, and she heard to her joy that most of it had been transferred to the banker Torlonia in Rome and to another banker in Leghorn. Her mother had only managed to bring some of her jewels; she now heard that the rest were safe in the hands of a friend. The news from France was good. The people had rallied magnificently to the Emperor, who was about to take the field in the Low Countries. She began to feel herself again, and discovered that Lucca seemed to be full of amusing people—Russians, English, Poles, the sort of international society she had found so entertaining in the many years she had spent wandering from one watering-place to another.

Suddenly the blow fell. One day in late June the Governor of Lucca presented himself. With scarcely disguised relish he announced that Napoleon had been defeated at Waterloo, had abdicated, and was in flight. She assumed that he would go into exile in England and thought of joining him. Then she heard the doom-laden reports of the final stages of the drama—his flight to Rochefort with a view to taking ship for the United States, the British squadron in the roads making escape impossible, the decision to throw himself on the generosity of the British Government and ask for passage to England in H.M.S. *Bellerophon*; and then the unbelievable, the outrageous, news that he was being sent as a prisoner to St. Helena.

On August 9 the *Northumberland* sailed on the 4,470-mile

voyage which was to land Napoleon on St. Helena sixty-seven days later. The news reached Lucca within a fortnight. All was lost. There was no haven except Rome, where Pius VII, always indulgent to this frail daughter, had extended a paternal welcome. On October 10 she and her suite went back to Viareggio, took ship for Civita Vecchia, and a few days later reached Rome.

19. Rome

1815-20

A WEEK AFTER SHE ARRIVED IN ROME PAULINE CELEBRATED, on October 20, 1815, her thirty-fifth birthday. She had less than ten years to live, all of them to be spent in Italy, in exile. This final decade of her life was the most pathetic, with the slow and inevitable decline of health and spirit, a period of remembering happier things and accepting a future that held no future. There was no rapid transition from happiness to misery, from well-being to premature decay. The seeds of her early decline had been implanted long before the fall of Napoleon, the cancer of melancholy was already gnawing at her gay and frivolous nature. In the same way the hard and brittle elements in Pauline's character took their time to mellow and soften. Despite the cataclysm, perhaps because of it, she was still capable of sustained and persistent effort on behalf of her material interests, and had by no means lost her love of comfort and elegance or her penchant for pleasure of a frivolous kind. Nor was her loyalty to the fallen Emperor, in whose fall she and the rest of the family were sharing, dimmed for one moment during the six years he spent on St. Helena.

The transition to new conditions of living may not have seemed so abrupt. Though misfortune kept striking at the door, the edifice of the new life in Rome seemed fairly secure. Madame Mère had arrived and taken up residence with her brother the Cardinal in the Palazzo Falconieri, bought by the far-sighted Fesch the previous year, and here Pauline went to stay. The Cardinal had been received by the Pope, who had called in person on Madame Mère. Most of the family were dispersed. Joseph was in the United States, his wife Julie in Switzerland. Elisa was still under detention in Brünn and not to be allowed till the following year to join Caroline in the Austrian city of Trieste. Jérôme, under the protection of the King of Württemberg, was living in Austria. Lucien and Louis alone were with Madame Mère and Pauline in Rome.

King Murat, after his defeat by the Austrians and flight from Naples the previous May, had tried without success to obtain through Wellington permission to come and live in England. In August he took refuge in Corsica, from where he launched one last desperate attempt to recover his kingdom. Sailing by night with two hundred men in five small sailing ships and a felucca, he was directed through the treachery of the pilot of the felucca into an ambush on the Calabrian coast and rapidly overwhelmed with his handful of supporters. After being beaten and kicked, he was cast into a piggery for the night, hauled up before a hastily assembled military tribunal, and shot.

Poor Joachim! Pauline mourned her gallant, generous brother-in-law, and even Madame Mère, who had deeply disliked him during his life, felt her rancour effaced by his death. Napoleon, when he heard the news of his death at St. Helena, said that there never was seen a more determined, fearless, brilliant leader at the head of cavalry. His political judgment was unequal to his military virtue, and ill-luck towards the end of his career followed on the heels of ill-judgment. Shortly before he set out on his last fatal venture, the Austrian Government had offered him honourable retirement in Austria, but he never received the message.

During these first months after the collapse the minds of the Bonapartes in Rome were full of Napoleon and his fate. They longed for news, but received none. It was not till the autumn of 1817 that the first authentic reports reached them through Napoleon's chamberlain, Comte de Las Cases, who had been expelled from the entourage. All they knew was that he was immured in a horrible little island ten miles long by six broad, "that black wart rising out of the ocean", two months' sail away at the other end of the world. Later on they heard the name of the house where he lived—Longwood, situated on a high rocky plateau above the eternal breakers and often shrouded in mist. In this small house he had five rooms for his own use. He was accompanied into exile by Las Cases and his fifteen-year-old son, Comte and Comtesse de Montholon and their little boy, General Bertrand (Grand Chamberlain) and his wife who had been with Napoleon at Elba, and General Baron Gaspard Gourgaud (*Officier d'Ordonnance*). The Bertrands lived in a small villa about a mile away at Hutt's Gate. The rest, with Marchand, crowded into Longwood.

Pauline found a natural distraction from her anxieties in making a determined effort to put her affairs in order. She had received a first payment for the sale of the Hôtel de Charost and arrangements had been made for the further instalments, due to run till the summer of 1816, to be received on her behalf by the banker Torlonia. Neuilly, confiscated by the Bourbons, had been damaged by Royalist and pillaged by British troops, but Michelot had succeeded in transferring most of the best furniture to the Hôtel de Charost, and some of this had now reached her in Italy, with some of her vermeil ornaments and her furs. She sold the vermeil to Torlonia and instructed Michelot to dispose of anything he could as quickly as possible. Considering the disastrous situation of the Bonaparte dynasty and the difficulty of communications, Pauline had not done badly for herself. The sale of the Hôtel de Charost to the British Government was what had really saved her and with this, and the disposal of valuables, she was far from being ruined. None the less the change was great from her former affluent state, and it was not long before she bethought herself of Camillo, the immensely wealthy husband with whom she had had nothing to do for four years. She had not forgotten that, under the marriage contract of 1803, Camillo had undertaken to allow her the use of half the Palazzo Borghese at Rome with a sum of twenty thousand francs a year for up-keep. Borghese, who was living contentedly in his palace at Florence with the charming Duchess Lante della Rovere, wished to have nothing to do with his wife, and refused her access to his Roman palace.

Pauline was not to be so easily deterred. The Palazzo Falconieri, though vast, was not large enough to hold Cardinal Fesch and his pictures, Madame Mère with her civil and religious attendants, and a Pauline used to living her own life. She appealed to the Pope to settle the dispute. Pius VII was fond of Pauline, and had, for the Bonapartes in general, an affection which is surprising in view of the treatment he had received at the hands of the Emperor of the French. He immediately appointed the Grand Inquisitor of the Holy Office to take charge of the matter. Monsignor Cuneo d'Ornano was sympathetic, and a Corsican to boot. Camillo, as he had often done in his past disputes with Pauline, wrote to her in such injudicious terms that it prejudiced the Grand Inquisitor against his case. In June 1816 the Holy Office pronounced in her favour, and authorised her to inhabit not only the Palazzo Borghese but two other Borghese houses as well, adjudicating a suitable income to be paid by the Prince for upkeep. She was also able to lay hands on some of the Borghese family jewellery.

The summer of 1816 thus found Pauline, by her own efforts and the help of the Pope, comfortably installed and well provided for in Rome. Relenting, perhaps, of the hard bargain she had driven, she wrote Camillo an affectionate and grateful letter. With her passion for acquiring property she proceeded to buy the Villa Sciarra at the Porta Pia. This charming small palace, which she renamed the Villa Paolina, became her favourite residence in Rome.

She began to revive the habitual pattern of her way of life—the alternating current of ill-health and social activity. After a cure at Lucca she returned ready to create a new life for herself in Rome. Italian society was aloof to the sister of the fallen Emperor. But there was a cosmopolitan society, of the kind Pauline had always found congenial, of which English visitors were the most prominent. With her talent for combining the useful and the agreeable, she threw open her house to the English, who were enchanted by the Princess and the welcoming atmosphere of the Villa Paolina where, rather than in her sombre

Palazzo, she received *en intimité*. Pauline, nothing if not thorough, had furnished the salons of the villa in mahogany in the latest London style. For Lady Morgan, the Irish novelist, the Villa Paolina was a place "where English neatness, French elegance and Italian taste are most happily united". She went to one of Pauline's *déjeuners*, and found herself in "a circle composed of British nobility of both sexes, of the Roman princes and princesses, German grandees and American merchants—a singular congress. The collation was of sweetmeats, ices, light wines, coffee; and the principal amusement looking at the elegant apartments of the villa, sauntering in the gardens, and visiting some antiquities within the walls. It is the most hospitable house in Rome."

Many prominent Englishmen were loud in their criticisms of the Government for its inhuman treatment of the fallen Emperor. It was a topic which the opposition used to belabour the Government, and in distant St. Helena Napoleon's suite did all they could to stoke the fires. From the out-of-date copies of *The Times* which reached them from Plantation House they could follow pretty well the state of opinion in Europe. Napoleon enjoyed these intrigues on his behalf, though as a realist he can have set little store on the prospect of their resulting in anything. "However unhappy he is here," Gourgaud told one of the Allied Commissioners, "he secretly enjoys the importance attached to his custody, the interest that the Powers take in it." Napoleon heard that his sister was seeing a lot of the English in Rome, and understood. The French Ambassador, the Duc de Blacas, was furious and blacklisted the English visitors who frequented Princess Borghese. Her most ardent swain, the fifty-year-old Marquess of Douglas, was an unabashed admirer of Napoleon, who authorised the painter David to present the Duke with a copy of the portrait of him in his workroom at the Tuileries.

The English visitors, and not only ardent Bonapartists like Lord Douglas or Lord Holland, but women of the world like Lady Granville, found Pauline adorable. Pauline herself knew that her looks were fading. Illness and anguish had taken their toll, and she was nearing forty. When the Duchesse d'Abrantès came to see her in Rome in 1817, she could not conceal her consternation at the change in her childhood friend. "You find me very much changed, don't you?" remarked Pauline dolefully, as she lay, wraithlike and febrile, on her chaise-longue. She sent Laurette to look at Canova's famous reclining statue which was locked up in the Palazzo Borghese and occasionally shown, on permission from Camillo. Laurette's expression told her enough. She wrote to Camillo early in January 1818. "I know," she wrote, "that you occasionally allow my statue in marble to be seen. I should be glad if that was no longer allowed—because of the nudity of the sculpture which borders on indecency. It was only made to give you pleasure. Since that is no longer the case, it is right that it should be removed from view. Think from time to time of your devoted Pauline B."

Laurette, seeing the statue again after all these years, thought it an admirable masterpiece. "The flesh is nature itself. *Morbidezza*, so sought after by sculptors, was there in all its voluptuous perfection." Pauline knew that the voluptuous perfection was there no longer.

In the spring of 1818 she went by sea to Lucca, accompanied for the last time by Douglas who was on his way home to England, where he was soon to inherit as Duke of Hamilton. On her return to Rome at the end of October she fell desperately ill from a gastric fever. In early December she thought she was dying and sent for Cardinal Consalvi. Ill throughout the winter, she gradually recovered and was persuaded by Madame Mère to come with her to Lucien's villa at Frascati instead of undergoing the exhaustion of her usual journey to Lucca and the rigorous treatment there. Pauline improved, but these were long months of invalidism. By her fortieth birthday in October 1820 the tortured constitution was desperately frail.

20. Bonaparte a passé par le tombeau
1821

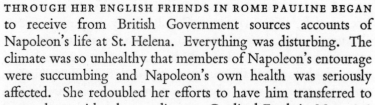

THROUGH HER ENGLISH FRIENDS IN ROME PAULINE BEGAN
to receive from British Government sources accounts of
Napoleon's life at St. Helena. Everything was disturbing. The
climate was so unhealthy that members of Napoleon's entourage
were succumbing and Napoleon's own health was seriously
affected. She redoubled her efforts to have him transferred to
somewhere with a better climate. Cardinal Fesch in May 1818
received an even gloomier account from General Bertrand.
Three members of the entourage had died. The unhealthy
climate, said Bertrand, affected Europeans particularly. Even
the natives rarely reached old age. He begged Fesch to obtain
permission for the dispatch of a priest "of our religion", who
should be under forty years old and a Frenchman or an Italian,
a good cook and a French doctor of established reputation.
Fesch approached the Pope, with whose help the necessary permission was obtained from the French and British governments.

Pauline offered her own chef, Chandelier, who had worked
in the Imperial kitchens in Paris and was known to be completely
devoted to the Emperor. Fesch himself, in consultation with his
sister, chose the other two. As priest, he selected an aged Corsican abbé, Buonavita, who had never worked in France, only
in Spain, Mexico and Paraguay. He had recently had an attack
of apoplexy and was sometimes unable to express himself. But
he had been almoner to Madame Mère, and both she and Fesch
insisted that his disabilities and age were outweighed by his
courage and devotion. For the doctor's post Fesch made an even
more unsuitable selection. Antommarchi, another Corsican, was
an anatomy specialist with scanty general knowledge of medicine.

The British Government, following these arrangements with attention, was told that Antommarchi possessed great talent for intrigue but little medical knowledge.

Napoleon and his entourage were aghast when the half-paralysed abbé and the ignorant doctor presented themselves at St. Helena at the end of September 1819. Napoleon welcomed the faithful cook, but he soon fell victim to acute rheumatism and had to be sent home.

Pauline was distracted with anxiety and frustration. She knew her mother and Fesch to be quite incapable of taking any proper action, living as they did in a haze of unreality and mysticism. They were under the influence of a German woman who had told them that the Emperor was no longer at St. Helena. The Cardinal was more or less out of his mind, going about saying openly that the Emperor was no longer there. Her uncle had concealed letters received from St. Helena, and actually made out that the silence proved his point. Her mother believed that the angels had wafted Napoleon to some other country where his health was excellent and from where she and the Cardinal received reassuring bulletins.

It was not till the Abbé Buonavita arrived in Rome in mid-July 1821 that Madame Mère returned unwillingly to the world of reality. The Abbé, who had left St. Helena on March 17 and had been delayed in England, went round at once to see Fesch and Madame Mère. Pauline happened to call just after the Abbé's arrival in order to say goodbye to her mother before leaving for a visit to Frascati, and learnt from the porter that Buonavita was in the house.

"I went up. Mama said nothing, and I was obliged to tell her that I knew the Abbé was there and that I wanted to see him and have news of the Emperor.

"Mama and my uncle do not entirely believe that the Abbé Buonavita left the Emperor at St. Helena, for they kept saying: 'I don't believe it at all, I know the Emperor isn't there any more.'

"I threw myself at Mama's feet, explained she was the victim

of an intrigue, and implored her to send that woman away. She
was furious . . . My uncle supported her . . . It was only after a
terrible scene that she began to be shaken. The scene was so
violent that I have broken with the Cardinal to the point of
never seeing him again."

She had her way and was allowed to see the Abbé. He handed
her a letter from the Comte de Montholon, dated March 17,
the day the Abbé had left St. Helena. It indicated plainly that
Napoleon was dying. His digestion had broken down completely and he could scarcely take any nourishment. He was
desperately enfeebled.

Pauline took instant action, and wrote to the British Prime
Minister, Lord Liverpool. Enclosing a copy of Montholon's
letter, she requested that Napoleon should immediately be moved
to a better climate. "If this request were refused, it would be
a sentence of death, and I beg you to allow me to go to St.
Helena so as to be with the Emperor on his death-bed. I know
that Napoleon's days are numbered, and I would never forgive
myself had I not used all means in my power to ease his last
hours and prove my devotion to him."

She added, pathetically, that as the state of her health did
not allow her to travel overland (the old malaise brought on by
the movement of a carriage), she proposed to sail from Civita
Vecchia to England, from where she would take the first available
ship to St. Helena.

Madame Mère, at last facing reality, also addressed Lord
Liverpool as well as a number of other persons in authority. By
the time he received these appeals, indeed before the time they
were penned, Lord Liverpool already knew that Napoleon was
dead. It was known in Rome on July 16. He had died at
Longwood at 5.50 p.m. on May 5.

For Pauline, all was finished. While she was writing, plead-
ing, planning, Napoleon had been dead, unknown to her,
across the vast expanse of the oceans. She vowed never to
receive an Englishman in her house again.

21. Farewell

June 9, 1825

LIFE FOR PAULINE, AS SHE HERSELF RECOGNISED, LOST ITS
meaning after Napoleon's death. After his final fall from power
her world had crashed about her, the world of the Empire in
which she had a place. But so long as he was alive his mere
existence, even in inaccessible St. Helena, gave a point, a
continuity, to her own. "I cannot visualise never seeing him
again," she wrote to Louis's wife, Queen Hortense, "and I am
desperate."

She was forty. Life somehow had to be faced, and Pauline
struggled on for four more years, concerning herself with her
health, indulging her passion for changes of scene, and expending
her last energies on trying to extract money from Camillo
Borghese.

During these years she continued to go to Lucca to take the
waters and also liked in winter to visit Pisa with its mild climate.
Near Lucca she bought a villa, the Villa Arnolfini which, like
the one at Porta Pia, she re-named Villa Paolina. Thinking of
the happy months she had spent with Napoleon on Elba and
remembering Viareggio, the little port from where she had
sailed to the island, the idea came to her of building a villa at
Viareggio. This likewise was christened Villa Paolina. The
villa of San Martino at Elba was hers too, left to her by Napoleon
in his will.

There was still a spark of flirtatiousness left in her. The last
love of her life, Giovanni Pacini, a Sicilian composer whose
operas were rivalling Rossini's, had been introduced to her a
few months before Napoleon's death. He became a familiar of
her house in Rome and followed her in her pilgrimages to

Lucien's villa at Frascati, to Pisa and to her villas at Lucca and Viareggio. The ambitious and gifted young man (he was fifteen years younger than Pauline) found her amusing and useful. She created a musical salon around him, which brought him to notice in Roman society and enabled her to live among the artists and entertainers to whom all her life she had turned for distraction. The Villa Paolina at Rome became a centre for local and visiting musicians. Its atmosphere was that of the light-hearted, half-serious, sophisticated gatherings which Stendhal, friend of Rossini and Donizetti, so much enjoyed in the Roman world of pleasure and intrigue.

Lady Bessborough, who had not seen Pauline since the heady winter of 1802 in Paris when Bonaparte's star was rising, found her still pretty, surrounded by a bevy of Cardinals. Lady Morgan, too, noted that "since the days of Pope Joan, no lady was ever so attended by Cardinals as the beautiful Pauline".

In the New Year of 1823 she recaptured, for a moment, the past and Napoleon. A young man, Jean-Jacques Coulman, presented himself at Pisa with a letter of recommendation from the Comte de Las Cases, who had been with Napoleon at St. Helena at the beginning and had just published his memoirs, the *Mémorial de Sainte-Hélène*. Coulman read out to her the passage in which Napoleon referred to her: "Pauline, the most beautiful woman of her day, always was and will be to the end the best creature in the world."

She wept uncontrollably on hearing this voice from across the oceans of the past. She was enfeebled and ill. Her sorrows and experiences, as Coulman noted, had used her up and parched her. Her figure was still elegant, her expression kind and full of character. But her complexion had become yellow and bloodless.

She caught his glance. "It is since his death that I have lost my health. I suffer, as he did, from my liver. He says I was the most beautiful woman of my day. Oh, dear! That was never so. But once I looked better than I do now."

She avidly asked for news of her friends in Paris, the only

place where she really cared to live and which, she knew, she would never see again.

Her salon, her travels, her new acquaintances helped Pauline to forget and to make life just bearable. But they cost money, as did the villas at Lucca and Viareggio. Her mind turned to Borghese, but she had seen nothing of him since she came to live in Italy; he had prudently put a certain distance between himself and Pauline and was living in Florence, in great contentment, with his Italian duchess. A change at the Vatican, with the death of Pius VII in September 1823, gave her the idea of reopening the settlement of 1816.

She brought a suit against Camillo in the Rota, and, confident of success, assumed her money troubles to be at an end. To her astonishment and dismay, the suit failed. She did not know where to turn to finance her numerous establishments. As if this was not enough, Pacini was betraying her. At first she could not believe it, though he seemed to be avoiding her and on one occasion she caught him out in a patent falsehood. Then a letter from Jérôme, who had run across Pacini in Trieste, left her in no doubt. She asked a mutual friend to tell the faithless musician that her decision was irrevocable; she would not answer his letters, which would be returned unopened.

This, as Pauline herself wrote, was the decisive act which at last would bring her peace of mind. It was as if she had written *"Finis"* to her *vie galante*.

These two events—the rupture with Pacini and the failure of her attempt to obtain an income from Camillo—occurred simultaneously in the late summer of 1824. To Pauline, in her debilitated state of health, this meant the end of living and the end of loving, the end in fact of life. Her letters began to be desperate and one at least of her correspondents, Cardinal Rivarola, was sufficiently disturbed to approach Pope Leo XII on her behalf. The Pope decided to take action. He wrote a firm but persuasive letter to Prince Borghese, pointing out how irreligious it was for a good Catholic, especially when he was a Roman prince, to live apart from his wife. He summoned the

Prince to recall his wife, live with her in peace and harmony and thus set an example to Christendom.

Camillo knew that beneath the pious phrases there lay the sanction of authority. He knew that he was bound to conform. But at least he could lay down his conditions. Assuming that the Pauline he was asked to take back was the Pauline of her feckless heyday, and thinking of his own peace of mind, he stipulated that if he was to be reconciled with her, she must get rid of the *"bande de comédiens"* with whom she lived surrounded.

Poor Pauline! She was ready to agree to anything. She no longer had the heart or the health for joyous living. She accepted at once, and hurried to join him at Florence.

The last six months of her life have the artificiality of an epilogue. She became a model wife and Camillo suddenly found himself a devoted husband. The irony of the situation must have appealed to her capricious nature. She discovered that life after all was worth living. Florentine society, buzzing with excitement at the news of the arrival of the famous, the notorious princess, could hardly believe their eyes as they saw Prince Borghese driving with his wife in the Corso, and escorting her to the opera. Pauline even summoned up strength during the winter season to give a number of receptions in the Borghese palace, with Camillo at her side.

It was the final effort, and in April she took to her bed, with six doctors around her. They could do nothing for her. She wrote to Louis, who had been to see her: "I am still very ill, worse in fact than when you left. I am always being sick, and am in continual pain." The Florentine palace was noisy—"they are putting down new paving stones in the street," she told Louis, "and the noise of banging is unbearable." She was grateful when Camillo rented first one, then another villa in the country-side outside Florence. At the Villa Strozzi, one morning in early summer, she knew she was dying. It was June 9, 1825. Perfectly lucid and composed, she sent for the family lawyer and in the presence of five witnesses, including her brother Jérôme, dictated a long will, disposing of her property and possessions in a most judicious way to her relations and descendants. Joseph received nothing, "because he has no need of anything"—presumably because she considered him well able to make his way in America, where he had gone to live on the collapse of the Empire in 1815. Lucien, surprisingly, nothing. Her ladies-in-waiting and attendants were remembered, together with Duchand who had saved her fortune, and Pacini, her last lover, his faithlessness forgiven at the end.

To Camillo she left the Villa Paolini at Lucca "as a slight recognition of the sincere and true attachment he has shown towards me during my long illness". Slowly dictating, she paused and added firmly: "I recognise that though circumstances and events may have temporarily divided us, Prince Borghese always conducted himself with the greatest loyalty and fidelity towards the Emperor, my brother."

The King of Rome must be appropriately remembered, the Emperor's son by Marie Louise. He was fourteen, growing up, and would soon need a house of his own, some refuge from the forbidding vastness of Schoenbrunn. What better than the charming little villa at Elba with the Egyptian hall and the Pompeian bathroom which the boy's father had built on ground she herself had bought and which he had willed to her in his testament? Yes, it was a special pleasure to leave San Martino to Napoleon's son, and she could not know that he was never to leave Vienna, where he was virtually a prisoner and was soon to die.

It was the final act, in the grand manner of a member of a royal house of France. At the very end she came to the disposal of herself.

"I do not wish to be exposed in the apartments, as is the custom. I desire to be embalmed and taken to Rome, which is my domicile, to be placed in the church of Santa Maria Maggiore, in the Borghese chapel. I die a prey to the cruel and horrible pains of a long illness . . . I die without feelings of hatred or animosity towards anyone."

Pauline

The dictation had taken most of the morning. When it was completed, she sank contentedly back on the pillows. At one o'clock Camillo closed her eyes. He saw that her last instructions were carried out, transported her the next day to Rome and placed her in the chapel at Santa Maria Maggiore, between the two Borghese popes.

THE END

APPENDIX

Pauline's Paris house 150 years later

MANY OF MY PREDECESSORS HAVE RECORDED, IN LETTERS
or memoirs, the convenience and elegance of the house in the
Faubourg St. Honoré. There was every reason, under the
Bourbon Restoration, to exploit its possibilities for resplendent
occasions. The costume ball given in 1829 by Lord Stuart de
Rothesay, the Charles Stuart who preceded and followed the
Duke of Wellington and who had been raised to the Peerage in
1828, was long remembered, especially the moment when the
Ambassadress paused on the grand staircase attired as Mary,
Queen of Scots. But even Lady Stuart was eclipsed in her
enjoyment of opening the house to the French courtly and
official world and British residents in Paris by Lady Granville,
whose husband, alternating with Lord Stuart de Rothesay, had
three tours as Ambassador between 1824 and 1841. She too gave
a ball, in the New Year of 1826. "My house looks more brilliant
and enormous than I can describe . . . We opened the *rez-de-
chaussée* . . . I have asked eleven hundred and fifty." A few days
later she confessed: "I can't make my accounts come right."

The cost of candles was a constant worry. Gas lighting was
not installed in the Embassy till 1852, though the Chancery had
that advanced form of lighting as early as 1825.[1] Today, when
the ground floor is opened for large parties, the Empire candelabra, the same as those which Lady Granville used, are still filled
with candles. According to a charming tradition, an incoming
Ambassador is "received with candles". Nobody who has
enjoyed this experience will forget the beauty of the effect of

[1] For these and many other details concerning the history of the building
since its purchase in 1814 I am obliged to Dr. R. D. Middleton.

207

candlelight reflected in the mirrors as he passes through a series of gilt and brocade Empire drawing-rooms.

This historic British possession, the first Embassy to be owned by a British Government, is still as conveniently situated, close to the Presidential palace (the Elysée) and the Ministry of Foreign Affairs (the Quai d'Orsay) as it was in the days of Napoleon I or Napoleon III. It is ideally adapted for an Ambassador to carry out his duties, whether receiving French guests from all walks of life in an essentially French setting with decided British overtones, or working at his desk—the Duke of Wellington's desk. For the Ambassador's official staff, however, up to the Second World War the Embassy was extremely uncomfortable. As early as 1842 there were complaints about the inadequacy of the accommodation for the secretaries, who worked in the pavilion or gate-house to the west of the main gateway (the stables and carriage-house in Pauline's time). The Ambassador of the day (the first Lord Cowley) suggested that the Government should buy the adjoining Hôtel de Commaille to serve as offices. The suggestion was sharply rejected and the Chancery, despite recurrent complaints, continued to be housed for another hundred years in the gate-house. In 1947 the next-door house was bought and modernised except for one floor of ornate Second Empire rooms, providing excellent office accommodation for the enlarged staff of modern days.

The interior of the Embassy today is much more like Pauline's house than it was in Victorian days, when the Empire furniture was replaced by contemporary bric-à-brac or covered by studded fabrics in the Victorian style. Of course, neither the Victorians nor the Bonapartes were able to obliterate the early eighteenth-century character of the house. The grander the room, the less the temptation to tinker with the original style; the great central *salon* on the ground floor has remained more Louis XVI than Empire. What Pauline achieved was a harmonious union between tradition and the *nouvelle vague*, replacing the furnishings of Louis XV and Louis XVI but making few and restrained changes in the friezes and overmantels and retaining the chandeliers and the general eighteenth-century style of the rooms. The Victorians banished the Empire furniture and replaced silk wall-coverings with panels plastered with pictures.

The process of restoring the house, after the Victorian transformations, to its Empire appearance in an eighteenth-century frame has been long and slow. It started at the beginning of the present century when King Edward VII, a frequent visitor, took a personal interest in the house. In succeeding years many original pieces of Empire furniture were recovered from cellars and attics, repaired and grouped together; the silk wall-coverings were reproduced with the original Napoleonic designs, first by French and—since the end of the last war—English weavers. The work of restoration continues. Today the tenant of Pauline's house lives in an interior very like the one she created in what, in her time, was the new fashion. Running water was introduced into the house in 1880, though the kitchens had been joined to the mains as early as 1785, and electricity was installed in 1896. Despite modern central heating, the reception rooms in winter still rely for warmth on logs (and candles). There are two lifts; one of them is only suitable to carry logs from the basement to the reception floors. The kitchens, originally in the pavilion opposite the old Chancery building, were moved in 1909 to their present position adjoining the main house, thus reducing the distance to the main dining-room from sixty to a mere thirty yards.

In the nineteenth century there were constant and frequently acrimonious disputes between the Ambassador of the day and the Government about repairs and their cost. In 1835 Palmerston, considering that almost £33,000 had been spent on repairs since the purchase of the house twenty-one years earlier, refused to sanction further expenditure and decided that it should be sold. Lord Granville successfully contested the decision. In the 1850's, during the second Lord Cowley's mission, a large-scale scheme of repairs and modernisation was undertaken. Parliament called for a report. The Office of Works sent out an architect to conduct a survey. He found the roof leaking and the house generally in a deplorable condition. He estimated that £20,000 would be required to put it in order. His report caused an outcry. The idea of spending money on the upkeep of national property abroad was repugnant. It was evidently thought that a house in France could somehow look after itself.

The present decorations of the ball-room and state dining-room date from the 1850's. Queen Victoria, while in Paris in August 1855, approved what was being done, as the Prince Regent had endorsed the original purchase and as King Edward VII was to encourage the restorations which make the house the stylistic *chef d'œuvre* that it is today. It was during his reign that the small salon on the first floor, a billiard room in Pauline's day, was arranged as a dining-room—an inestimable benefit to subsequent Ambassadors who, until then, had been obliged either to use the vast state dining-room on all occasions, or entertain guests in the eighteenth-century manner in one or other of the reception rooms as weather or fancy dictated.

Reading the impressions left by his predecessors over the past 150 years, the modern tenant of the British Embassy in Paris cannot fail to be forcibly struck by the fact that, for all the changes of historical circumstance and material convenience, the purpose and function of this stately house have been consistently the same. Apart from its prime function as headquarters for the conduct of British relations with France, with its blend of the styles of the two nations, it has proved its worth as a forum where French and British can meet and both feel at home, and as a focus for the British community in France and visitors from across the Channel. However, the range of activities of the Ambassador and his staff have changed with the times. There are fewer balls and more business lunches—though the Parisians of the Fifth Republic seem to enjoy a ball at the British Embassy as much as they did in the days of Charles X. Another difference arises from the rapidity of modern communications. A modern Ambassador in Paris rarely spends more than a month on end in his Embassy. He and his staff nowadays travel widely, thus improving their knowledge of France, getting to know the French people better, and keeping in touch with the British consulates in the provincial centres.

There is no doubt that the central part of the job of the Ambassador to France lies in Paris and always will, however tempting the lure of travel made easy by modern communications. The British are fortunate in being housed in an Embassy well suited for the conduct of relations with their closest neighbour and one which retains all the character of a particularly vital period of French history.

Sources and Authorities

THE BRIEF, TRAGIC AND ADVENTUROUS LIFE OF PAULINE Bonaparte and the contradictions in her character have attracted many biographers, mostly French. I have listed those biographies I have found most reliable, omitting others which are less useful owing to an uncritical acceptance of the veracity of anything that was alleged against her. Admittedly a controversial figure in her own day, she was often the victim of jealousy on the part of her contemporaries or of the running stream of anti-Bonapartist propaganda from which no member of the family escaped. I am particularly indebted to Joachim Kühn's *Pauline Bonaparte*, a detailed and precise narrative of the vicissitudes and peregrinations of Pauline's restless life, written when he was a member of the German Embassy in Paris before the Second World War.

Since French books were more accessible, I have sometimes used French translations of English publications.

Apart from the *Mémorial de Sainte-Hélène*, I have found the Memoirs of Méneval, his secretary, the most illuminating of contemporary sources for an understanding of Napoleon's way of life. The Memoirs of Constant, the valet who deserted in 1814, were not written by Constant himself, and though vivid, are full of back-stairs gossip which needs to be treated with reserve. Those of Marchand, who succeeded Constant and was with Napoleon at Elba and St. Helena, are of a different order and unreliable only to the extent that the writer's loyalty sometimes made him uncritical.

On the Bonaparte family, and indeed on Pauline herself, Frédéric Masson's monumental work in thirteen volumes, *Napoléon et sa Famille*, dry and dispassionate, is indispensable. Of contemporary memoirs, those of Pauline's childhood friend, Laure Permon, later Madame Junot and Duchesse d'Abrantès, give the most striking picture of life under the Consular and Imperial courts, though many

Sources

of her judgments (especially on Pauline) need to be accepted with caution. The letters of Lady Bessborough, another gifted observer, published by Castalia Countess Granville in *Lord Granville Leveson-Gower. Private Correspondence 1781 to 1821*, give an excellent picture from an English viewpoint of Paris during the rise of Napoleonic power.

The descriptions of Pauline's Paris house in the rue du Faubourg St. Honoré are based on my own observations, and details of the purchase by the Duke of Wellington in 1814 are taken from the collection of the Duke's papers published by Colonel Gurwood. (*The Dispatches of F. M. the Duke of Wellington*, vol. VII. See also A. Detrez, *Le Faubourg Saint-Honoré*.)

CONTEMPORARY CORRESPONDENCE AND MEMOIRS

ABRANTÈS, DUCHESSE DE (Madame Junot), *Memoirs of Napoleon, his Court and Family*, English translation, London 1836
Histoire des Salons de Paris, Paris 1836–8

ARNAULT, A. V., *Souvenirs d'un Sexagénaire*, vol. III, Paris 1834

BEUGNOT, JACQUES-CLAUDE, *Mémoires du Comte Beugnot, publiés par le Comte Albert Beugnot, son petit-fils*, 3 vols., Paris 1866

BIANGINI, FELIX, *Souvenirs, publiés par Maxime de Villemarest*, Paris 1834

BOSWELL, JAMES, *The Journal of a Tour to Corsica*, ed. S. C. Roberts, London 1929

BOURRIENNE, LOUIS-ANTOINE FAUVELET DE, *Mémoires de Monsieur de Bourrienne sur Napoléon*, 10 vols., Paris 1829

CAMPBELL, SIR NEIL, *Napoleon at Fontainebleau and Elba*, London 1869

CONSTANT, (CONSTANT WAIRY) *Mémoires de Constant sur la vie privée de Napoléon, sa famille et sa cour*, 6 vols., Paris 1830

COULMAN, JEAN-JACQUES, *Réminiscences*, 3 vols., Paris 1862–9

FOUCHÉ, JOSEPH, DUC D'OTRANTE, *Mémoires*, ed. L. Madelin, Paris 1945

GIRARDIN, STANISLAS DE, *Mémoires, Journal et Souvenirs*, Paris 1834

Sources

GOLDSMITH, LEWIS, *Histoire Secrète du Cabinet de Napoléon Bonaparte et de la Cour de Saint-Cloud*, London and Paris 1814

GRANVILLE, CASTALIA COUNTESS (ed.), *Lord Granville Leveson-Gower. Private Correspondence 1781 to 1821*, 2 vols., London 1916

LAS CASES, EMMANUEL, COMTE DE, *Mémorial de Sainte-Hélène*, 10 vols., Paris 1823
Napoléon à Sainte-Hélène, Paris 1913

LECESTRE, LÉON, *Lettres Inédites de Napoléon I* (An VIII-1815), 2 vols., Paris 1897

LEVESON-GOWER, F., *Letters of Harriet Countess Granville*, 2 vols., London 1894

MARCHAND, LOUIS JOSEPH NARCISSE, *Mémoires de Marchand, publiés d'après le manuscrit original par Jean Bourguignon*, 2 vols., Paris 1952

MÉNEVAL, N. JOSEPH DE, *Méneval's Memoirs of Napoleon I*, translated by H. Sherard, 3 vols., London 1894

NAPOLEON, *Correspondance de Napoléon Ier* (published under instructions from Napoleon III), 28 vols., Paris 1858–69

NORVINS, M. DE. *Histoire de Napoléon*, Paris 1839
Mémoires, publiés par L. de Lanzac de Laborie, Paris 1897

RÉMUSAT, MADAME DE, *Mémoires, publiés par Paul de Rémusat*, 3 vols., Paris 1880

STENDHAL (HENRY BEYLE), *Promenades dans Rome*, 2 vols., Paris 1855
Vie de Napoléon, ed. Louis Royer, Paris 1929
Mémoires sur Napoléon, ed. Louis Royer, Paris 1929

VILLEMAREST, MAXIME DE, *Le Piémont sous l'Empire et la Cour du Prince Borghèse. Souvenirs d'un Inconnu.* (Vol. VI of Constant's *Mémoires.*)

MODERN BIOGRAPHIES OF PAULINE BONAPARTE

ALMÉRAS, HENRI D', *Une Amoureuse. Pauline Bonaparte*, Paris 1916

AUGUSTIN-THIERRY, A., *Notre Dame des Colifichets. Pauline Bonaparte*, Paris 1937

GOBINEAU, MARCEL, *Pauline Borghèse, Soeur Fidèle*, Paris 1958

Sources

KÜHN, JOACHIM, *Pauline Bonaparte*. Traduit de l'allemand par G. Daubié, Paris 1937

NABONNE, BERNARD, *Pauline Bonaparte*. *La Vénus Impériale*, Paris 1963

TURQUAND, JOSEPH, *Les Soeurs de Napoléon*, vol. I, *Les Princesses Elisa et Pauline*, Paris 1927

GENERAL HISTORIES AND LIVES OF NAPOLEON

ARTHUR-LÉVY (Lévy, Arthur), *Napoléon et la Paix*, Paris 1902

AUBRY, OCTAVE, *Sainte-Hélène*, 2 vols., Paris 1935

BAINVILLE, JACQUES, *Histoire de France*, Paris 1924
Napoleon, London 1932

CAMBRIDGE MODERN HISTORY, vol. IX: *Napoleon*, Cambridge 1907

FISHER, H. A. L., *Bonapartism*, Oxford 1908

GAVOTY, ANDRÉ, *Les Drames Inconnus de la Cour de Napoléon (Les Trois Maris d'Eléonore)*, Paris 1964

IUNG, THEODORE, *Bonaparte et Son Temps*, 3 vols, Paris 1880

JOHNSTON, R. M., *Napoleon, a short biography*, London 1904
The Corsican. A Diary of Napoleon's Life in his own words, London 1910

Larousse du XXe Siècle, publié sous la direction de Paul Augé, 6 vols., Paris 1928–33

LÉVY, ARTHUR (Arthur-Lévy), *Napoléon Intime*, Paris 1893

LOCKHART, J. G., *The Life of Napoleon Buonaparte*, London 1897

LUDWIG, EMIL, *Napoleon*, English translation, London 1927

MALET, ALBERT, *XVIIIe Siècle, Révolution, Empire*, Paris 1918

MARKHAM, FELIX, *Napoleon*, London 1963

MASSON, FRÉDÉRIC, *Napoléon et sa Famille*, 13 vols., Paris 1898–1929
Napoléon et les Femmes, Paris 1894

NICOLSON, HAROLD, *The Congress of Vienna*, London 1946

ROSE, J. N., *Life of Napoleon I*, 2 vols., London 1910

THOMPSON, J. M., *Napoleon*, Oxford 1952

Sources

OTHER BOOKS CONSULTED

ANDREWS, WAYNE, *Germaine. A Portait of Madame de Staël*, New York 1963

BINDOFF, S. T., and others, ed., *British Diplomatic Representatives, 1789–1852*, London 1934

CASTRIES, DUC DE, *La Conspiration de Cadoudal*, Paris 1963

DECAUX, ALAIN, *Letizia, Mère de l'Empereur*, Paris 1949

DETREZ, ALFRED, *Le Faubourg Saint-Honoré*, Paris 1953

DUFF COOPER, A., *Talleyrand*, New York and London 1932

GIAFERRI, PAUL LOUIS DE, *L'Histoire du Costume Féminin Français*, Paris(?) ca. 1910

GURWOOD, COLONEL, *The Dispatches of F. M. the Duke of Wellington*, vol. VII, London 1844–7

IUNG, THEODORE, *Lucien Bonaparte et ses Mémoires (1775–1840)*, 3 vols., Paris 1882

KNAPTON, ERNEST JOHN, *Empress Josephine*, Cambridge, Mass. 1963

KURTZ, HAROLD, "Madame de Staël and the Duke of Wellington, 1814–1817". Article in *History Today*, November 1963

LEROUX-CESBRON, C., *Le Château de Neuilly*, Paris 1923

MASSON, FRÉDÉRIC, *Joséphine, Impératrice et Reine*, Paris 1899

STIRLING, MONICA, *A Pride of Lions. A Portrait of Napoleon's Mother*, London 1961

VACQUIER, J., *Les Vieux Hôtels de Paris. Le Faubourg Saint-Honoré*, Paris 1913

WILLIAMS, H. NOEL, *Madame Récamier and her Friends*, London and New York 1901

WILSON, BECKLES, *L'Ambassade d'Angleterre à Paris*. Traduit de l'anglais. (*The Paris Embassy*), Paris 1929

WILSON, R. MCNAIR, *Joséphine. The Portrait of a Woman*, London 1929

Germaine de Staël, London 1931

Index

In the index, Pauline is referred to as P., Napoleon as N., and the name Bonaparte as B.

Index

Index

Index

Index

Index